D1067689

Live Zen

Extemporaneous talks given by Osho at the
OSHO International Meditation Resort, Pune, India

OSHO

LIVE ZEN

A NEW THERAPY IS BORN:
THERAPY THROUGH GIBBERISH

Editing: Khumal
Design: Haritomedia.com
Typesetting: Abhay
Production: Kamaal

Published by OSHO Media International, 17 Koregaon Park, Pune 411001 MS, India

Photos: Courtesy OSHO International Foundation, Haritomedia.com

The material in this book is a transcript of a series of original OSHO Talks Live Zen given
to a live audience. All of Osho's talks have been published in full as books, and are also
available as original audio recordings. Audio recordings and the complete text archive
can be found via the online OSHO Library at www.osho.com/library

Printed in India by Thomson Press (India) Ltd., Mumbai

ISBN 81-7261-207-9
ISBN 978-81-7261-207-8

Osho comments on excerpts from Two Zen Classics: Mumoukan and Hekiganroku,
translated by Katsuki Sekida, © Katsuki Sekida and A.V. Grimstone. Reprinted by
arrangement with Shambhala Publications inc., Boston, MA. www.shambhala.com

**DEDICATED TO THE SUCHNESS
OF EVERYTHING**

CONTENTS

PREFACE

To say it in words has not been the way of Zen. It attracts people, takes away their ideologies, their theologies, their religions. It leaves you absolutely fresh at the very center of your being. Without saying anything, you experience the mystique, you experience the mystery of existence and life.

But because it is an experience – in Zen they don't even use the word *experience*, they use the word *experiencing*, because the experience is not something dead and complete. It is a river flowing, flowing, alive, moving.

The word *experience* indicates that it has become complete. Anything that becomes complete becomes dead, and Zen is the most alive thing in the world; hence it cannot be said that it is an experience. We have to invent a word, *experiencing*; instead of river, *rivering*. That gives the clear-cut idea that a river is not static, it is moving – on the way, always on the way, moving eternally, falling into the ocean, rising into the clouds, falling in the rain on the mountains, and again into the river…moving in a circle of tremendous aliveness, never stopping anywhere.

There is no full stop in Zen, and all our words – experience, knowledge, understanding – give the illusion of a full stop. We have to change our nouns into verbs – verbs come closer to life. We use the word life, but we should use the word living – that comes closer. Moment to moment, living. Life seems to be something dead; it has already completed its course, has come to an end, to the graveyard.

Zen is certainly a mystique. In fact, it is the only mystique there is. But it is not being said, it is kept a secret so that you don't go inside your being with a certain idea. You go absolutely clean and fresh. You will find the mystery, the immense mystery of life, but Zen's absolute approach is not to give you any idea what you are going to find.

Osho

The Zen Manifesto: Freedom from Oneself

NOTE TO THE READER

At the end of each chapter there is a guided two-stage meditation. The first stage is sitting in absolute silence, as if "frozen." After two minutes the participants allow themselves to fall to the floor in total relaxation before Osho calls them back.

In the last talk of this series Osho introduces a new stage to the evening meditation. Each stage of the meditation is preceded by a signal from Osho to the drummer, whom he calls by name.

The drumbeat is represented in the text as follows:

The first stage is gibberish, nonsense language, which Osho describes as "cleansing your mind of all kinds of dust…speaking any language that you don't know…throwing all your craziness out." Gibberish helps us break the habit of continually "rationalizing" and "verbalizing" our unconscious turmoil.

The gibberish is represented in the text as follows:

ishtrciamistrasimbaworrrastaba
cosiiiusmarpatokulospos SHARNAS
MBHALASRHADDABASLAMKAMALKALEJAKAM
σηαβνασιτιασκι λυλαβελαβαλλαβαρ
wiurnci LULABELABALLABAR
khelkerstakciciuntopenjdt tjkn khjjknhhuzdqugfurrlasma
sleikniylokjdlaih
srubbililisisrirtra Jkn kjikpoonolo gerrastas
washugtu

The second stage is a period of silent sitting, of entering inward to the center, witnessing. Osho often says a few words during this stage to help us go more deeply into this witnessing.

The third stage is "let-go." Each person falls effortlessly backward, "like a bag of rice" or "a falling tree" – and lies on the floor as if dead." In Osho's words:"die to the world, die to the body die to the mind so only the eternal remains in you."

A final drumbeat is the signal to "come back to life and return to a sitting position." At this point everyone is invited by Osho to take this witnessing consciousness with them into their everyday life – as an undercurrent running twenty-four hours a day.

The entire text of each gibberish and let-go is reproduced here, and one of these is always included at the end of the daily Evening Meeting at the OSHO International Meditation Resort in Pune, India.

EMPTINESS, NOT HOLINESS

1

Osho,

Emperor Wu Asks Bodhidharma
Emperor Wu of Liang asked Bodhidharma, "What is the first principle of the holy teachings?"
Bodhidharma said, "Emptiness, no holiness."
"Who is this standing before me?"
"No knowing."
The emperor did not grasp his meaning.
Thereupon Bodhidharma crossed the river and went to the land of Wei.

The emperor later spoke of this to Shiko, who said, "Do you in fact know who this person is?"
The emperor said, "No knowing."
Shiko said, "This is the Bodhisattva Kannon, the bearer of the Buddha's Heart Seal."
The emperor was full of regret and wanted to send for Bodhidharma, but Shiko said, "It is no good sending a messenger to fetch him back. Even if all the people went, he would not turn back."

Setcho put it like this:

The holy teaching? "Emptiness!"
What is the secret here?
Again, "Who stands before me?"
"No knowing!"
Inevitable, the thorns and briars springing up;
Secretly, by night, he crossed the river.

All the people could not bring him back.
Now, so many years gone by.
Still Bodhidharma fills your mind – in vain.
Stop thinking of him!
A gentle breeze pervades the universe.

The master looks around:
"Is the Patriarch there? – Yes! Bring him to me,
And he can wash my feet."

Osho,
This verse seems to contain the essence of Zen –
"No knowing." Is this why you have called Zen the
only living religion?

M aneesha, before you asked the question, the trees have
heard it.

It is one of the most fundamental things to be remembered by all of you that a religion is living only when there is no organized doctrine, no system of beliefs, no dogma, no theology. When there is just this silence and the trees enjoying the dance in the breeze, in your heart something grows. It is your own, it does not come from any scripture; nobody can give it to you because it is not knowledge.

That is the greatest difference between all the religions on one side and Zen on the other side. All religions except Zen are dead. They have become fossilized theologies, systems, philosophies, doctrines, but they have forgotten the language of the trees. They have forgotten the silence in which even trees can be heard and understood. They have forgotten the joy that has to be natural and spontaneous to the heart of every living being.

The moment the experience becomes an explanation, an expression, it breathes no more; it is dead – and all over the world people are carrying dead doctrines.

I call Zen the only living religion because it is not a religion, but only a religiousness. It has no dogma, it does not depend on any founder. It has no past; in fact it has nothing to teach you. It is the strangest thing that has happened in the whole history of mankind – strangest because it enjoys in emptiness, it blossoms in nothingness. It is fulfilled in innocence, in not knowing. It does not discriminate between the mundane and the sacred. For Zen, all that is, is sacred.

Life is sacred whatever form, whatever shape.

Wherever there is something living and alive it is sacred.

Today we are beginning to discuss a few incidents in the long history of Zen – which are unique because no other religion exists on anecdotes. They are not holy scripture; they are simply incidents that have happened.

It is up to you.

If you understand them they can open your eyes and your heart. If you don't understand them nothing else will ever be able to open your eyes and your heart. And what I am saying is categorical, absolute.

These small anecdotes in their very smallness just like dewdrops contain the whole secret of the ocean.

If you can understand the dewdrop there is no need to understand the ocean you have understood it.

Please be very silent and careful.

Emperor Wu of China asked Bodhidharma... Fourteen hundred years before, Bodhidharma had gone to China. He was a unique man: his statements, his actions, his behavior, all contained the pure essence of religion. But he was not a professor, he was not a missionary. He was a man who was ready to share his being with you without holding anything back – but you have to be ready to receive it.

Naturally, Emperor Wu asked Bodhidharma,

"What is the first principle of the holy teachings?"

That's how other Buddhist monks had described it to him. But Bodhidharma was not an ordinary Buddhist monk; in fact, he has nothing to do with Buddhism. He is his own self – he belongs to nobody. It is just a coincidence that his master happened to be a Buddhist. He himself never said that he was a Buddhist; he could not commit such a great stupidity.

You will see that the man was almost a lion and his words were just like the roar of a lion. Those who have seen Bodhidharma were blessed people and those who understood him, there is no way to define their gratitude. He was not a man of many words; he was very telegraphic. He did not use a single word more than needed. He did not care about language; he did not care about the emperor.... He cared only about the truth – that it has not to be spoiled by any description, that it should be kept clean and pure.

Bodhidharma said, "Emptiness, no holiness."

Do you see the telegraphic language? He has been asked by Emperor Wu the first principle of holy teachings and he is saying emptiness is the first, but don't call it holiness – there is no holiness. When everything is holy what is the point to call something holy? Categories are possible only when something can be unholy.

To the experience of the awakened there is only nothingness so pure, so lovely so beautiful.

But it is difficult to call it *holy* because that beautiful word has been corrupted by the religions, by creating a fictitious entity: *un*holiness. Just to make somebody a saint they have made the whole of humanity sinners.

The reality is: there is no saint and there are no sinners; there are only people who are asleep and there are only people who are awake. The difference is so small that just a little ice-cold water thrown into your eyes – and the difference disappears.

"Emptiness, no holiness" – and Bodhidharma has said all that can be said. In fact he has said even that which cannot be said; his teaching is complete. He has come to the full point in a single sentence – not even a complete grammatical sentence, but just a hint: *"Emptiness, no holiness."*

Emperor Wu was one of the greatest emperors of China, a very cultured man. It hit him very strongly. He never expected that anybody should misbehave in front of the great emperor. And this man does not even say, "Your Holiness" or "Your Highness." He does not even address the emperor. All that he says is: *"Emptiness, no holiness."*

Certainly he must have been angry inside; it is natural – he had been waiting for three years. Bodhidharma took three years to reach – and he had heard so much about the man and the man seems to be a very strange fellow, a little weird. Offended but not showing it, behaving like a cultured, sophisticated hypocrite, he again asked,

"Then who is this standing before me?"

If the first principle of existence is emptiness and there is nothing holy, then who are you, who is this standing before me?

Great was Bodhidharma. I cannot conceive of anybody else in his place when I see his answer. It is simply just his own, absolutely authentic. He does not bother that the emperor is offended – he offends even more. But what he says is such a great truth that he is not responsible.

Truth always offends.

That's why truth is always crucified.

He simply said,

"No knowing."

The emperor had asked, *"Who is this standing before me?"* and Bodhidharma said, *"No knowing."* He does not even use the word *I*. You simply see the beauty of the man and his utter commitment to truth – that he will not descend even a single step so that he can be understood. Understood or not his commitment is to the truth, not to any emperor.

Whenever I have come to this point I feel we need many Bodhidharmas in the world – such integrated people, so uncompromising, so fearless and so devoted to the truth. His truth is that he does not know who is standing before Emperor Wu. He is saying exactly what Socrates said in his last days: "I don't know anything." But still Socrates was using the word *I*, he was not of the category of Bodhidharma. See the difference: he says, "I only know that I know nothing," but the I remains and this knowing that "I don't know anything" remains.

With Bodhidharma, everything has been dropped. He is saying, "In front of you is standing no knowing, just pure innocence."

> The emperor did not grasp his meaning.

Obviously it would have been difficult for anybody to grasp the meaning – unless one has already grasped it, but then he would not have asked.

Seeing that the emperor did not grasp his meaning,

> Bodhidharma crossed the river and went to the land of Wei.

That was out of the territory of the emperor.

> The emperor later spoke of this to Shiko...

another Zen master

> ...who said, "Do you in fact know who this person is?"
> The emperor said, "No knowing."
> Shiko said, "This is the bodhisattva Kannon, the bearer of the Buddha's Heart Seal."
> The emperor was full of regret and wanted to send for Bodhidharma, but Shiko said, "It is no good sending a messenger to fetch him back. Even if all the people went, he would not turn back."

A man like Bodhidharma never turns back: what is past is past; you cannot bring him back into the past. You miss the opportunity, nothing can be done about it.

Another Zen teacher – not a master – has put the anecdote in this way:

> The holy teaching? "Emptiness!"

This is the way of teachers. This is not a lion roaring, this is a schoolmaster, a mouse creaking like the trees...

> The holy teaching? "Emptiness!"
> What is the secret here?
> Again, "Who stands before me?"
> "No knowing!"

He is simply repeating what he has heard; he has not understood it himself.

Inevitable – but he makes commentaries on it!

> Inevitable, the thorns and briars springing up;
> Secretly, by night, he crossed the river.
>
> All the people could not bring him back.
> Now, so many years gone by,
> Still Bodhidharma fills your mind – in vain.
> Stop thinking of him!
> A gentle breeze pervades the universe.
>
> The master looks around...

I will not say *the master* because I cannot agree with him. I can accept at the most that the schoolteacher looks around and repeats something which is fashionable in Zen circles:

"Is the Patriarch there?"

The Patriarch – he is referring to Bodhidharma. The founders of Zen are called patriarchs...

"Is the Patriarch there? – Yes! Bring him to me,
And he can wash my feet."

Now he is trying to pretend that he understands the strange ways of Zen. He is also making a strange statement: *"Bring him to me, and he can wash my feet."*

It is simply ugly. Schoolmasters should not enter into the area of truth. Their world consists of small, borrowed knowledge to transfer. They should not speak as if they are lions, because they are not. He has not added a single word to make Bodhidharma's statement more understandable; he has not given any transparency to it. He has not made Emperor Wu understand what not knowing is – he is a pretender.

This man's name is Setcho. Many times in these commentaries we will come across people who are only teachers but are pretending to be masters. But you should understand that the anecdote is so complete....

Only if you look into my eyes perhaps you may find the commentary or if you look into my empty hands you may find the meaning.

What Bodhidharma has said is absolute, complete. Nothing can be added to it and nothing can be deleted from it. Even a Gautam Buddha would have been surprised by the flowering of Bodhidharma. He is saying that all is empty and unless you enter into emptiness you will not understand anything of life and its mysteries. And nothing is holy, so don't be bothered to become saints, discipline

11

yourself, practice this or that.

Just enter into your own being.

In the silences of the heart nothing is missing.

The saint is just pretending – because the reality is already there. It needs no practice, no holiness.

All that it needs is awakening.

Just wake up and just see who is within you.

It does not mean you will come to know great knowledge, it does not mean that you will come to know who you are. It simply means you will come to know that there is pure innocence. That is your essential being, and in it nothing is holy.

A beautiful rose is beautiful, but do you think there are saintly roses and sinner roses? Except the priests who have dominated man, the very categories of the sinner and the saint do not exist in existence. *All* is beautiful, tremendously graceful – but there is nothing holy. And when you enter into yourself, you will even have to leave the idea of I outside. Without leaving the idea of I, you cannot enter within yourself.

The "I" is your ego. It is the barrier, not the bridge.

That's why, instead of saying, "I don't know," which would have been more grammatical...but a man like Bodhidharma does not care about grammar.

Do you think I care about grammar?

Bodhidharma simply says, *"No knowing"* – and he has said everything; he has not left anything.

I am reminded of a story...

Gautam Buddha is passing through a forest, it is fall time and dry leaves are falling and making great noise dancing in the wind all over the place. Ananda asks him, "I don't interfere because there is always somebody else who is asking you; it is a great opportunity for me that by chance I am alone with you. I want to ask one thing; I have been resisting but now I cannot resist. I want to know whether you have told us everything that you know, or you have told only some things."

Gautam Buddha bent down; he plucked up a few dry leaves in his hands and he said, "Ananda, do you see these dry leaves in my hand? This much I have said to you. And look at the dry leaves all over the forest: this much I have not said to you. Because you cannot understand even this much, these few leaves in my hand. It will be absolutely a wastage of time to talk about all the leaves of this forest. My knowing is vast; I have just given you a taste."

But if by chance Bodhidharma had been asked, his answer would have been diametrically opposite. He would have said, "I have said everything, I have not been keeping anything to myself" – and that's why he is not understood. He has said too much. His words are so condensed that just this simple phrase, *"No knowing"* can contain thousands of scriptures. Still it will remain not understood.

Bodhidharma's uniqueness is that he does not care about anything else, he has no other considerations. Only one other man, George Gurdjieff, would have agreed with him. In the whole history of great masters only George Gurdjieff used to teach his disciples: Do not consider. Do not compromise. Let the truth be as it is; you cannot make it better. You cannot paint it, you cannot give it a little more color, a little more joy, a little more expressibility; you cannot do anything.

If you know it your eyes will be just like empty sky. Your hands will not be like fists holding something, but empty indicating that there is nobody inside but a pure nothingness.

But this pure nothingness is alive, this nothingness has a heart. This nothingness blossoms in thousands of flowers and rainbows, and dances in peacocks, and sings in birds. This nothingness roars in the oceans and this nothingness is silent in the meditator.

This nothingness, remember, does not mean what you ordinarily understand by nothingness. It is better to break the word in two. When Bodhidharma uses *nothingness* he simply means no-thingness. Just put a little hyphen – and you have made Bodhidharma more understandable. I cannot do more than that. Just a little hyphen: nothingness becomes no-thingness. You are a living entity, not a thing.

Emptiness does not have the negative connotation that it carries in our minds. When I show you a room which is completely empty, there are two ways to say something about it. Either you can say that the room is empty or you can say that the room is full of space. Exactly the very word *room* means space. The more furniture you bring in the less room there is. You can fill the whole room with junk and the room disappears. It is there and it is not there. You cannot throw it out, but you can hide it behind your furniture, behind your refrigerator, behind your television. Take them all out...what remains? Roominess, emptiness; in a positive sense, a pure space.

So remember, when Bodhidharma says emptiness, he does not mean your idea of emptiness. His emptiness is immensely full; his emptiness is immensely positive. His nothingness is simply no-thingness; his denying knowing is simply affirming innocence.

It is a wonder that in two small statements he has revealed the very heart of religiousness.

Osho,

Bokushu's Empty-Headed Fool
Bokushu asked a monk, "Where are you from?"
The monk gave a "katsu" shout.
Bokushu said, "This old monk is shouted down by you."
The monk shouted again.
Bokushu said, "What about the third and fourth
shouts?"
The monk stayed silent.
Bokushu hit the monk and said,
"You empty-headed fool!"

Setcho put it like this:

Two shouts, three shouts;
the knowing one knows well;
if going hell-bent,
both are blind.
Who is blind? Fetch him!
Expose him to the world!

Osho,
I also am an empty-headed fool – I don't understand this sutra at all! Could you give the fifth
shout?

Maneesha, it is a beautiful koan. Bokushu is one of the
great Zen masters.
He asked a monk,

"Where are you from?"

This is always asked by the Zen masters when a new disciple comes. And just by the answer of the disciple it is decided whether he is going to be accepted as a disciple or thrown out. It is immensely important, it is not just a sociability, not a kind of introduction.

When Bokushu asked the monk:

> "Where are you from?"
> The monk gave a "katsu" shout.

Just as you say "Yaa-Hoo!" – it is a shout, without saying anything but making it clear that: "I am here and it does not matter from where I come. What kind of nonsense question are you asking? I can come from anywhere – that does not matter. What matters is: I have come."

The shout is to declare that "I am here and you are asking stupid questions… Ask something about me! Don't waste time."

But Bokushu was not to be satisfied so easily, because it has now become traditional. So when the master asks – although you don't understand what you are doing – you can give a shout. It is known; it is written in the scriptures – thousands of incidents. But you cannot cheat a man of the quality of Bokushu.

> Bokushu said, "This old monk is shouted down by you."
> The monk shouted again.
> Bokushu said, "What about the third and fourth shouts?"

Now he has created trouble.

He has never heard about the third and fourth. The first

and second shouts have become traditional by the time of Bokushu, and a master's function is to cut through the tradition. So he said, "Okay, okay, these shouts are okay, just tell me about the third and the fourth."

> The monk stayed silent.
> Bokushu hit the monk and said,
> "You empty-headed fool!"

Zen is strange – nowhere else in the world has anything like this happened. The monk, the stranger, remaining silent gave the answer. He could have shouted a third time, he could have shouted a fourth time, a fifth time...what is the problem? But rather than shouting a third and fourth, he simply remained silent. He is saying, "Don't waste time. As far as the game, the traditional game is concerned, it is enough; now silence is my third and fourth shout." And only in Zen would it be possible that *Bokushu hit the monk and said, "You empty-headed fool!"*

It is acceptance. He has been accepted as a disciple because of his silence. To hit him is to accept him, and to call him *"You empty-headed fool"* is a very affectionate expression. It is almost saying, "Sweetheart, my darling." It is not rejection. In those two shouts he followed the tradition, but he would not go on repeating the tradition; he gave his own shout, and that was silence.

Bokushu hit the monk and said, "You empty-headed fool!" In Zen an empty-headed fool is almost ready for meditation. A man full of knowledge is far away from meditation. An empty-headed fool is simply a loving way of saying that you are not far away from becoming wise.

The fool can become wise; the knowledgeable never. The

empty-headed can become empty-minded, but the man who is carrying scriptures and degrees and the universities and the libraries in his head, he is far away. A master will not unnecessarily waste time on such a person.

The anecdote is complete, but the same schoolmaster, Setcho, puts it like this:

> Two shouts, three shouts;
> the knowing one knows well;
> if going hell-bent,
> both are blind.
> Who is blind? Fetch him!
> Expose him to the world!

It is sheer stupidity. I am afraid we will have to meet this fellow Setcho again and again. Schoolmasters should not enter into the lion's den, but this Setcho has entered; now I cannot save him.

Maneesha, you say, "I also am an empty-headed fool – I don't understand this sutra at all! Could you give the fifth shout?"

We will – we give it every day! We are going to spread the shout all around the world. It will be heard on every street, in every house.

But it is good that you understand yourself also as an empty-headed fool. I don't hit people, but Niskriya…hit Maneesha. Do it!

[*Niskriya, the video cameraman, is sitting exactly behind Maneesha. He gets up and kisses Maneesha softly on her head.*]

It is enough of serious thinking – the trees don't like it! And I always listen to the trees. Look, they have become silent....

A young porter in Washington is brought to court for raping one of the maids.

The maid alleges that she was leaning out of the window to watch the President of America drive along the street below in a parade. The porter lowered the window on her, trapped her, and had his way with her.

"But, Miss," says the judge, "why did you not start screaming?"

"What?" cries the horrified girl, "and have everyone think I was supporting Ronald Reagan?"

Olivia Oppenheimer is a very rich widow, who has a parrot called Percy, who can talk and sing in four languages.

Percy is a huge hit at parties and Olivia adores him. But Percy has one weakness: he loves to fly over the fence and fuck the neighbor's chickens.

Olivia tries everything to cure Percy of his habit, but with little success. Finally, she gets a pair of scissors and clips all the feathers off the parrot's head.

"There," she says, "that will teach you. Now all the lady chickens won't think you handsome anymore!"

Two nights later, Olivia has a party. Percy, the parrot, is in his usual spot on the piano as the guests come in.

Half way through the party, two bald men arrive.

"Hey!" calls out Percy. "Get over here with me, you two chicken-fuckers!"

A young Indian brave, son of Chief Running Bear, asks his father one day how he decides what names to give his sons.

"Simple," says Running Bear, "while I am making love, I look around and if I see an eagle circling in the sky, I call the child Flying Eagle, if I see a horse going by, I call the child Running Horse. It is just a question of what catches my attention while I am making love to your mother. So, now do you understand, Broken Condom?"

Now two minutes for absolute silence, no movement... closed eyes, just as if you are absolutely frozen.
Collect the whole energy inside.

Now relax...let go!

Now, come back to life.

NOT GOING ANYWHERE 2

Osho,

Joshu's The Real Way Is Not Difficult
Joshu spoke to the assembly and said, "The real way is not difficult. It only abhors choice and attachment. With but a single word there may arise choice and attachment or there may arise clarity. This old monk does not have that clarity. Do you appreciate the meaning of this or not?"
Then a monk asked, "If you do not have that clarity, what do you appreciate?"
Joshu said, "I do not know that either."
The monk said, "If you do not know, how can you say that you do not have that clarity?"
Joshu said, "Asking the question is good enough. Now make your bows and retire."

Setcho says:

The real way is not difficult.
Direct word! Direct speech!

One with many phases.
Two with one.

Far away in the heavens the sun rises, the moon sets;
Beyond the hills the high mountains, the cold waters.

The skull has no consciousness, no delight;
The dead tree sings in the wind, not yet rotten.

Difficult, difficult!
Attachment and clarity; watch, and penetrate the secret!

Osho,
In life one continually has to make practical decisions
– about how one will use one's time and energy, with
whom one will keep company, what one will eat....
Is there a difference between making choices,
judging and discriminating?

Maneesha, we are reaching to the second greatest Zen master, Joshu. Nothing can be compared with Bodhidharma, but if anyone else comes close to him, that is Joshu. But he just comes close, not to that height, not that Everest, but one cannot do anything about it.

Some trees grow very high, some trees don't. In the world of trees there is no comparison.

In the world of real consciousness, authentic realization, also there can be no comparison. But still one should not forget the highest, so that one does not become lost into the thousand and one great peaks.

The Himalayas are thousands of miles. Each peak is unique has something to say, has some beauty to reveal, some truth...stands on its own feet, not dependent, not imprisoned, with tremendous glory and splendor.

One can easily get lost and I would like you to remember the highest, because that should be your aim too.... Your arrow should point to the highest.

Before I say something about Joshu, I would like to remind you of Bodhidharma's sutras that we discussed yesterday. In just a very few words he has condensed the whole experience, the whole interiority, the whole kingdom of God: "Emptiness, nothing holy." And when the emperor asked, "Then who is standing before me?" the answer was, "No knowing."

Yesterday I forgot a very special point to be made to you that will give you the taste of real Zen. He said, *"No knowing."* He could have said, "Not knowing," but he chose, "No knowing," because "not knowing" implies the existence of I. No knowing does not imply; it simply states innocence. Not knowing is ignorance and no knowing is innocence.

Such is the clarity and depth of this man Bodhidharma. Even Socrates said, "I do not know anything." Even he falls far below the heights of Bodhidharma. He accepts in his statement the existence of I; he accepts the existence of knowledge. He is simply saying, "I am ignorant."

Just a little difference, how small and how delicate: no knowing – not knowing. A small letter "t" and worlds are set apart.

In these fourteen centuries that have followed Bodhidharma, hundreds of Zen masters of great clarity, insight, awakening, have happened, but no one even comes close to the depth, the subtlety, the beauty and the immense perception of Bodhidharma. As I look into Bodhidharma, I don't find any other single individual in the whole history of mankind – Gautam Buddha included – who can be said to have condensed religion into its simplest possibility, expressed religion into its absolute purity. It is obvious that this man is going to be misunderstood, condemned, ignored. The greatest peak of consciousness that man has achieved, mankind has not been kind enough to remember it. Perhaps there are heights our eyes cannot reach, but we should try our best; one never knows.

Just a few days ago China discovered a higher peak of the Himalayas than Everest. For centuries Everest was the highest peak; it is no longer so. It is good that Edmund Hillary is dead; otherwise in his old age he would have suffered very much. He has enjoyed the great success of reaching to the highest peak of Everest. But fortunately before China's discovery he was dead.

It is possible that some day someone may reach to a higher consciousness than Bodhidharma. It has not happened for fourteen centuries, but that does not mean it is absolutely decisive. I don't see any difficulty, because the sky is infinite. Just a little more courage, a little more understanding, a little higher flight and you can reach to the joy that has been up to now only Bodhidharma's.

I would love my people to remember it, that there is no limitation, no boundaries, no hindrances – there are skies upon skies. As long as you want you can fly, you won't touch the boundary of the universe. There is no such thing, no boundary line.

It has been very difficult for scientists to accept the idea that the universe is unbounded. Obviously it is difficult even to conceive of something that has no boundaries. One tends to think that somewhere, very far away, millions or trillions of light years away, but there must be a boundary! Mind can accept any boundary anywhere, but the reality is that by its very nature, existence cannot have any boundary, because what will be beyond the boundary? – again another sky. That's why I am saying skies upon skies are available for your flight. Don't be content easily. Those who remain content easily remain small: small are their joys, small are their ecstasies, small are their silences, small is their being.

But there is no need. This smallness is your own imposition upon your freedom, upon your unlimited possibilities, upon your unlimited potential.

Bodhidharma is a milestone, but the way goes farther, always farther.

Joshu says:

"The real way is not difficult."

Our minds say that spiritual growth is very difficult. Our religions make it as difficult as possible. According to them it takes many, many lives to reach to your own self – how ridiculous, how stupid! If I am to reach to myself…in fact I will tell Zen Master Niskriya to give a good Yaa-Hoo hit to Joshu.

Niskriya…

[*Niskriya is dressed up as a zen monk and has cut his hair very short. He hesitates over what to do.*]

Give it without any fear.

[*Niskriya gets up.*]

Where is your staff?

[*To everybody's astonishment, he produces a long wooden staff.*]

Right! You have the staff. Good.

Whom do you think to hit?

[*Niskriya hits his own head with the staff. Osho laughs and signals to him to sit down again.*]

Good.

The real way is not difficult, because there is no way. You are already where you have always been and will always be. What nonsense to talk about *The Way!* That's why I said that, although Joshu is second in the hierarchy of Zen he has not that magic, that touch. That has been monopolized by Bodhidharma.

Even to talk about the way is to make things difficult. I absolutely agree with Joshu that the way is very easy, but I cannot agree with his expression in the way I can agree with Bodhidharma, with absolute synchronicity, as if I have spoken those words myself: Emptiness, nothing holy, no knowing.

With Joshu I can only sympathize. I will not say he is wrong, but I will certainly say that the moment you start talking about the way, it becomes difficult. It becomes difficult because from here to here, there is no space for the way. If you are going somewhere else a way is possible – difficult or easy, it depends. But if you are not going anywhere, but simply being yourself, here and now....

Joshu needs a good hit.

By chance today Master Niskriya is dressed up exactly, but Joshu is not here. But wherever Joshu is, and whoever the people are who believe in Joshu's enlightenment, Master Niskriya's hit will reach. I am using Master Niskriya's hit because I am a very nonviolent person; moreover, so lazy that I have dedicated my whole function of hitting people to Master Niskriya. And he really looks...he is not only dressed up, at this moment he *is*. It is another matter that the next moment he may forget.

This moment you are also just emptiness.

No knowing.

Pure innocence.

But to go on remembering it is the only problem. You don't have to do anything, except to continue to remember that you are where you are, that you are what you are; that whatever you do, you can never be anywhere else, anybody else; that in this simple acceptance of your being, you have achieved all that has been achieved by the great buddhas.

There is no question of way; hence I can say that Joshu has a little understanding, but not much. He says, *"The real way is not difficult."*

> Joshu spoke to the assembly and said,
> "The real way is not difficult.
> It only abhors choice and attachment.
> With but a single word there may arise choice and attachment or there may arise clarity.
> This old monk does not have that clarity.
> Do you appreciate the meaning of this or not?"

If you accept the basic assumption that there is a way – it is only a hypothesis – then Joshu is right that the only things that can prevent you from reaching it are judgment, choice, attachment. *"With but a single word there may arise choice and attachment or there may arise clarity. This old monk..."* – he is referring to himself – *"This old monk does not have that clarity."* Only on this point does he reach a height, accepting that *"This old monk"* – he is not using the word *I* – *"this old monk does not have that clarity. Do you appreciate the meaning of this or not?"*

He is asking the assembly of the other monks.

Before I discuss the answers of other monks, I would like to repeat again that fundamentally Joshu is absurd. There is no way; hence, the question of its difficulty or easiness does not arise. Because there is no way, there is no question of choice, choicelessness, judgment or no judgment, clarity or cloudedness.

So remember – I was not in the assembly of Joshu, unfortunately, but time makes no difference. What I could not say in his assembly, I am saying in my own:

The way exists not. You are the very goal.

Now have a look to the assembly of Joshu's disciples...

> Then a monk asked, "If you do not have that
> clarity, what do you appreciate?"
> Joshu said, "I do not know that either."

Again remember Bodhidharma saying that standing before you is no knowing. He does not even by implication allow the existence of an ego. Joshu does not have that penetration. He is far closer to Socrates. He says, *"I do not know that either."* He accepts the existence of "I" and he accepts the existence of ignorance. He misses the great peak of no knowing.

> The monk said, "If you do not know, how can
> you say that you do not have that clarity?"

These are tremendously beautiful dialogues. It is unfortunate that in our times there are no such assemblies; no such dialogues are happening, not even in our great universities. Everything has become so small, so mundane; everything has become so commercial.

The monk said to Joshu, *"If you do not know, how can you*

say that you do not have that clarity?" At least you know this much: that you don't have that clarity. The same would have been the situation of Socrates, but he was surrounded by very ordinary disciples. Joshu may not be right, but certainly he has great disciples.

The disciple is saying, "You say, I don't have that clarity – at least you have accepted that you know *something*. It is enough to show the contradiction."

> Joshu said, "Asking the question
> is good enough. Now make your
> bows and retire."

Not a great statement.... The monk, unknown, was far more clear than the master himself. And saying to the monk that, *"Now make your bows and retire,"* freaks me out! Joshu should have touched his feet and asked for forgiveness. He did not prove his steel.

Now again we have to listen to the schoolmaster Setcho.

Setcho says:

> The real way is not difficult.

This is what is called parrot thinking. Now what is the point to repeat it?

> The real way is not difficult.
> Direct word! Direct speech!

Now this idiot does not understand a word and he is saying that what Joshu has said is:

Direct word! Direct speech!

One with many phases.
Two with one.

Far away in the heavens the sun rises, the moon sets;
Beyond the hills the high mountains, the cold waters.

The skull has no consciousness, no delight;
The dead tree sings in the wind, not yet rotten.

Difficult, difficult!
Attachment and clarity; watch, and penetrate the secret!

There is no secret. Joshu's statement is simply without any reality in it, the question of any secret does not arise. But the schoolmaster tries to make it look as if there is some great secret. As a camouflage he writes some beautiful, poetic lines, but they have nothing to do with Joshu's remark. They are simply an attempt to express, to exhibit that "I am a man of great understanding, I know the secret; now you penetrate...." And there is no secret at all.

He reminds me of an old proverb...

In ancient Greece, in the times of Anagoras... Anagoras was one of the great predecessors of Socrates, not a great philosopher, but he became great because people poisoned him also. I have never talked about him because there is nothing much about him, but still – by poisoning him, people have put him in the same category as Socrates and Jesus. Anagoras used to say – and from him comes the proverb – that a philosopher is a blind man in a dark night, in a dark house, searching for a black cat which is not there.

Maneesha, you are asking: "In life one continually has to make practical decisions – about how one will use one's time and keep energy, with whom one will keep company, what one will eat…. Is there a difference between making choices, judging and discriminating?"

In ordinary life everything that you are doing is all right, but if you want to know the extraordinary livingness of your innermost core, then you will have to drop judgment, choice, discrimination. There is no need. In the inner world there is no marketplace, no shopping mall! In the inner world even you are not! Who is going to judge and what is going to be judged?

Again remember Bodhidharma:

Emptiness, nothing holy, no knowing.

I am not speaking on Bodhidharma, I am speaking of my own vision, which coincides with that of Bodhidharma.

It has been a serious evening with Joshu…. You have enjoyed the silence. Now I would like to disturb your silence a little as a preparation for a greater silence.

Pope the Polack is wandering through the Vatican gardens one day, when he nearly steps on a toad.

"Hey!" shouts the toad. "Don't pass me by!"

"What?" cries the startled pope.

"I am a human being," replies the toad, "who has been bewitched to look like a toad. Whoever saves me will have anything he wants."

"Well," replies Pope the Polack, "I always wanted to be

the most famous pope of all time!"

"Simple!" says the toad. "You take me to your bed, let me sleep on your pillow, and in the morning you will have a wonderful surprise!"

So Pope the Polack puts the toad under his huge pointed hat and smuggles it into his bed.

Just as the cardinal brings in the pope's early morning tea, the toad changes into a beautiful princess…. At least, this is the story the pope is giving to the newspapers.

The express train is crowded with businessmen on their way to the city. In a first-class carriage, Mr. Wong is sitting reading the *Beijing Times,* when a white-coated waiter comes along the passage with the breakfast trolley.

He stops by Mr. Wong, and says, "You for coffee?"

"No," snaps Wong, "I got first-class ticket. *You* fuck offee!"

Miss Goodbody's class goes for a picnic in the woods.

After all the kids have drunk lots of lemonade, several of the girls retire to the bushes to pee and there is trouble with the brambles and the nettles.

Little Ernie walks in amongst them, pulls out his pecker and pees without any trouble.

"Wow!" says little Sally, really impressed, "that's a handy thing to bring on a picnic!"

Mrs. Benzini has been visiting her psychiatrist, Professor Potts, for years and feels that she is not getting any better. One day, she decides to confront the shrink. "Doctor," she says, sitting up on the couch, "I come-a every week for five years. Nothing change-a. What's-a going on? You gotta tell me. What's-a wrong with me?"

"Well," replies Potts, "I will be frank with you. You are crazy!"

"What?" cries Mrs. Benzini. "Crazy? *Crazy*? I wanna second opinion!"

"Okay," says Potts, "you are ugly too!"

Now close your eyes…
Be absolutely still, as if frozen.

Now, relax.

Now, come back to life.

PECKING AND TAPPING   3

Osho,

Kyosei's Instructions on Pecking and Tapping
A monk said to Kyosei, "I want to peck from the inside.
Would you please tap from the outside?"
Kyosei said, "Could you attain life or not?"
The monk said, "If I could not attain life I would become
a laughingstock."
Kyosei said, "You too are a fellow in the weeds."

Setcho put it like this:

Old Buddha had his way of teaching,
The monk's answer won no praise.

Strangers to each other, hen and chick,
Who can peck when the tapping comes?

Outside, the tap was given;
Inside, the chick remained.

Once again the tap was given;
Monks throughout the world attempt the trick in vain.

Osho,
This anecdote evokes such a beautiful image of
what transpires between master and disciple.
Can you talk about the peck and tap that we call
our relationship with you?

Maneesha, before I talk about Kyosei and his statement, I am reminded of a very significant awakened man. He was a potter; his name was Gora. He uses this image very significantly, because when a potter makes a pot he has to do two things: inside he pecks and outside he taps. That is the whole art of pottery, but that's also the whole art of the master and disciple relationship.

Even though he became enlightened, Gora remained a potter. He inspired millions of people – very rich people, even the kings, were his disciples. And they again and again asked him, "This does not look good. You stop this business of pottery. We feel ashamed."

Gora said, "Even if I drop the visible business of making pots, what about my being your master? What am I doing with you? – pecking and tapping."

Yes, Maneesha, this is the whole art of the master. If he cannot peck from inside when he starts tapping from the outside, he will destroy the disciple. And most of the so-called teachers of the world exactly do that. They don't even know their *own* inside – how can they help somebody else's growth with this art of pecking from inside and tapping from outside?

Tapping from outside is very easy, even Zen Master Niskriya can do it. But the real question is the support from inside. Great things can be said to you which will not be of any help, which on the contrary may pollute you and poison you, because they will make you knowledgeable. A master is your enemy if he makes you knowledgeable. But from the outside only knowledge can be given. You become more and more filled with knowledge.

The real master has nothing to do with knowledge. He hits deep inside you. His compassion sometimes seems to be very hard, but he goes on showering from the outside, with great love. Inside he has to be a surgeon; outside he has to shower flowers of blessings. Unless a master can do both he is not a master, he is only a teacher.

> A monk said to Kyosei, "I want to peck from the inside. Would you please tap from the outside?"
> Kyosei said, "Could you attain life or not?"
> The monk said, "If I could not attain life I would become a laughingstock."
> Kyosei said, "You too are a fellow in the weeds."

Just as I have remembered Gora, the potter, Kyosei is

taking up a different dimension to it, the dimension of an egg. You can tap from the outside, but the bird inside the egg has to peck, himself. This takes Gora's explanation to a far deeper insight. A real master in fact need not peck you from within; your very life energy will do it. That's why Kyosei certainly and suddenly seems to be asking without any reference or context, "*Could you attain life or not?*"

He is saying, "As far as tapping is concerned, I am ready, but do you have energy enough to attain life? – because the other part, the pecking, you will have to do. You will have to take the risk to come out of the shell, to come out of the egg." Certainly, Kyosei far exceeds Gora's understanding.

The monk said, "If I could not attain life I would become a laughingstock."

He has understood why the master Kyosei is asking him, "*Could you attain life...?* Are you full of energy and abundance so that if I tap you, you will not be killed? Are you mature enough, centered, that my tapping from outside will not destroy you, but will give you the open sky, the freedom to fly? It all depends how much energy, how much life force you have. If you don't have that life, then you are only a fellow in the weeds."

No roses will blossom in the weeds. The weeds don't give any flowers, they don't have that abundance of energy that blossoms in a flower. A flower is a mysterious phenomenon. From the earth, you cannot find anything that resembles the rose that is going to grow out of it. Neither in the rosebush can you find anything resembling – even a faraway echo of the beauty, of the color, of the delicateness of a rose. It is not in the earth, it is not in the roots, it is not in the bush...but it has to be there, otherwise the flower cannot blossom.

The flower is an abundance of energy. Much energy is

used by the leaves and the foliage. Unless a plant has more energy than is absorbed by the foliage, by the branches, by the leaves, a rose is not possible.

The monk is right when he says, *"If I could not attain life I would become a laughingstock."* You tap the egg and you kill the bird inside by your tapping. The monk is saying, "I would be a laughingstock." And many disciples in the world...almost the whole world is in some way or other following a certain line of Hinduism, Buddhism, Jainism, Christianity without knowing they are disciples. But no roses blossom – they are all laughingstocks.

One Christian missionary, Stanley Jones, used to stay with me. He was a world-famous man. Six months he used to travel in the West to teach about Christianity, its theology, in the universities and six months he used to come to India. Whenever he was in my town, he used to stay with me. I asked him one day, "You have been a Christian for almost sixty years, but I don't see even a faint echo of a Jesus in you. You know much, but knowledge is not the thing. Your heart has not blossomed, your head is heavy. When are you going to grow roses?"

He looked at me a little shocked, because this is not the way of talking in any reference other than Zen. In every other religious context things are theoretical, philosophical, they are doctrines. Zen is not a doctrine. It is a very direct approach to the existential problem of why man has not blossomed, why millions of people have not grown roses in their gardens, why they are just weeds, laughingstocks.

Setcho comments on this small conversation. For the first time he is a little sensible. He is still a schoolmaster, but perhaps living in the company of the mystics, of the masters, he has learned something. I still suspect that it is only knowledge, but this time he comes very close to the truth. But remember, to be very close to the truth is still to be very far. Unless you *are* the truth there is no point in knowing how far you are from it. One mile, or one million miles, even a single inch, just a single word, and you have lost the truth.

Anyway, he has come very close. For the first time he shows the possibility; perhaps in the end he may turn into a roseflower himself.

Setcho says:

> Old buddha had his way of teaching.
> The monk's answer won no praise.
>
> Strangers to each other, hen and chick,
> Who can peck when the tapping comes?
>
> Outside, the tap was given;
> Inside, the chick remained.
>
> Once again the tap was given;
> Monks throughout the world attempt the trick in
> vain.

Just tapping from the outside is not going to help, unless the inner energy has become a tremendous longing to come out. Then, even without any tapping from outside the bird is going to break the eggshell by itself.

There have been many masters who had no masters. Their own longing for the truth was so tremendous they needed no help. Their own overflowing energy gave them the freedom to fly into the sky. The eggshell is very thin; it is not a China wall. You are not imprisoned in something made of steel; you are imprisoned in something made of thoughts. Such a thin rice paper, a Japanese curtain, that you can come out any moment you want. You don't have to wait for somebody to knock from the outside. And if you don't have energy, even if someone knocks it is not going to help.

There is a very beautiful poem of Rabindranath Tagore, "The King of the Night":

There is a temple devoted to the King of the Night – very ancient, huge, with one thousand priests. The high priest one night dreams that the King of the Night has appeared and said to him, "Tomorrow I am going to visit the temple. Clean it, prepare it. I have not been there for centuries. I have to go to many other temples too."

He woke up, perspiring, although he has been praying every day for just this fact, that "you should appear, you should give us a glimpse of your being, your splendor."

And now the dream has come, but a dream...? In the middle of the night, he called all the priests from their beds and said, "I am sorry to disturb you, but the problem is really serious. I have seen in my dream the King of the Night, saying, 'Prepare, clean the temple, I am coming to visit tomorrow.'"

The other priests started laughing. They said, "It seems you have become too old, senile. Just a dream and you have unnecessarily harassed us."

The old man said, "I understand that you will laugh at me. I thought about it before I woke you up, but there is no harm in preparing. Anyway the temple has needed painting for centuries."

The temple had been completely abandoned by people. It was far away from the habitation of people in the deep forest. And the priests had also by and by become skeptical. Many of them had stopped praying. Many of them had become agnostic: "Who knows if there is a King of the Night? We have been here – we have never seen him. Our parents have been here – they have never seen. Their parents have been here – they have not been able to see him. Centuries have passed and we have been serving these stone statues and now suddenly you want us to believe in your dream?"

The chief priest said, "I myself don't believe in it, but there is no harm. Just think of the other possibility if he comes… There is no chance, I know, but just give a one per-cent possibility. It is one hundred percent certain there is no possibility that he will come. It is just a dream, but just give one percentage point…if he comes and finds us unprepared, no flowers for him, no sweets for his welcome, no music, no dance, no candles, then we will be in really bad shape. One thousand priests…what are you doing here?

"And anyway, if we clean the temple, bring flowers, burn candles as if he is coming and he does not come, there is no harm. It is our temple and we live in it, we have celebrated it. The guest has promised but did not turn up. There is no harm in preparing, but in not preparing there is tremendous risk, and I cannot take that risk."

By that time the night was almost over and everybody gave thought to the old priest – he was reasonable. The temple was cleaned. It had hundreds of statues, so much dust, for centuries nobody has cared. They brought flowers and perfume, and they brought sweets and they prepared special food.

Half a day had passed and the suspicion started arising:

"Half the day has gone and he has not come yet. We are unnecessarily being bothered by this old fool's dream. Who has ever heard that any god comes to any temple? It goes against all factuality, all history, and we believed the dream and tired ourselves unnecessarily. And we cannot eat, unless the guest comes."

That is a simple rule in the temple. First the god has to be served and then the priests can share the food.

Up to now it had been easy, because the gods were only stone gods. Today was difficult. It was getting late, the sun had started going down and everybody was angry with the old priest: "We have wasted so much money unnecessarily on flowers, on painting.... We had to bring so many servants to clean, because it was almost impossible, it was so huge."

The old priest said, "I am sorry, but what can I say? He may still come."

The day passed and finally they decided, even against the head priest, "Now it is useless to wait – the sun has set. The whole day we have been hungry and working and now we are tired. We want to eat and go to sleep."

The old man said, "It is better just to wait one night more because he is the King of the Night – *that* we have forgotten completely. He will not come in the day; he will come in the night, if ever he comes."

They said, "Now we are no longer going to be persuaded by this stupidity to remain hungry and awake the whole night, waiting for your dream." They revolted.

The old priest said, "There is no need to revolt. I am myself old and tired and hungry; I will join you...perhaps it was just a dream."

And they all ate the delicacies they had arranged for the

god of the temple. They were so tired they fell asleep very soon, early in the night.

In the middle of the night came a golden chariot with the King of the Night, the god of the temple. The chariot came on the mud road leaving its marks on the mud up to the great gate of the temple. There were a thousand steps to reach to the temple, and the god of the temple climbed those thousand steps up to the main door.

The noise of the chariot on the mud road was heard. Some priest, half-awake, half-asleep said, "It seems he has come, because I hear the sound of a great chariot."

Somebody else shouted him down: "Don't disturb us now. Enough of all this nonsense! There is no chariot; it is just a cloud passing by."

Somebody else said, "But I have heard the steps – somebody is coming up to the main door."

Out of those thousand priests many jumped upon him and forced him: "Remain silent and quiet. It is nothing but a strong wind striking on the doors. Don't be deceived; don't think that the god will knock on the doors."

In the morning they were all crying because there were marks of footprints on those one thousand steps and on the mud road there were marks of a chariot, coming and going back.

The god had come – but they were asleep.

It is possible to find a master who can tap you, but if you are fast asleep, in your sleep you will find a thousand and one explanations and go on back to sleep. Perhaps it is a cloud, perhaps it is wind...you may find any reason to avoid; you will take another turn and go to sleep...nobody has come.

It all depends on your inner energy to be waiting at the

door for the guest to come, fully awake, in deep trust, in great love.

In fact your trust and your love are the constituents of the guest.

Your love creates, your trust creates – nobody comes.

Just your trust and your love blossoms and a fragrance surrounds you. Thousands of lights start burning around you.

It is *your* energy, your abundant energy – there is no other God.

Maneesha, you are asking: "This anecdote evokes such a beautiful image of what transpires between master and disciple. Can you talk about the 'peck and tap' that we call our relationship with you?"

In fact, the tap is not inevitable but the peck is inevitable. If you are overflowing with energy then even a man who knows nothing may give you a tap and you will be freed from your sleep, from your darkness, from your unconsciousness.

Once it happened with a great Tibetan saint, Milarepa.... He was a simple and innocent person and he followed a master who was not a master at all, but just a great scholar, very knowledgeable, had a great following. But Milarepa was not concerned with the knowledge. He loved the man, he trusted him. Although he was not trustworthy, he was not a master, Milarepa accepted him as a master to such an extent – the story is very beautiful, must be symbolic – that he would walk on water.

Other disciples who were older and senior to him could not do it; they tried. They asked Milarepa, "What is the secret?"

He said, "No secret; I simply trust my master. I remember

him and I say to him that I want to cross this river, that's all. I don't know how he manages."

Naturally, jealousy arose because he was a newcomer and he was suddenly becoming the most prominent because of his doings. He would jump from the mountains without being hurt…and the reason he would always give was, "It is my master."

It was reported to his master. The master was very much surprised. He himself would not dare to walk on water. He was a knowledgeable scholar, but that does not make you capable of walking on water. He could not jump from mountains into valleys without being hurt. But now he was in a difficulty. He could not say, "I am not responsible at all, it must be his own trust" – on the contrary he proved to be a very ordinary human being. He said, "Yes, it is my name and the power of my name."

So the disciples asked, "Then you show us: walk on the waters."

He said, "I will."

He thought in his mind, "If my name can manage it, then of course I am going to try it myself."

And after the first step he started shouting, "Help! Help!" because he was drowning. Somehow he was pulled out.

The disciples asked, "What happened?"

He said, "I don't know, I had never tried it before. Where is that Milarepa?"

Milarepa was on the other side of the river, so he came running on the water.

The master said, "My God, you have exposed me. I cannot do it, nor can my name do it; it must be your trust. It does not matter in what – in whom."

So once in a while it has happened that a master who was

not a master has helped somebody to become awakened, enlightened. And the contrary has also happened, that the master is fully awakened, he goes on shouting into your ears...but you don't think that you can fly, that the whole sky is yours, that you can be free from the imprisonment that you yourself have created of relationships, of success, of power, of prestige...thousands are the names of the devil, but the essential thing is that it imprisons you, it chains you.

It is in your power to break those chains, because those chains are made only of your imagination.

Maneesha, the most essential lesson on the path is of having a loving heart, of trusting the existence – of being in a let-go that if existence takes care of all this vast universe it will also take care of you. And whatever happens must be right because nothing can happen against existence.

This immense trust is difficult in the beginning, because you can't touch existence, you can't figure out what existence is.

The master is simply a very thin thread between you and existence. He can give you a tangible proof of trust and love. If he becomes the proof, the answer, then something in you will start opening up. The master does nothing, not even tapping.

So I am not in agreement with Kyosei and Setcho and Gora. What they are saying is significant but not significant enough.

The master does nothing.

His being a master is enough.

His silence penetrates the heart of the disciple.

There is no effort; it is just a happening.

The very presence of the master gives you the trust that life is much more than you have known up to now, much deeper, much vaster; that life is not just this mundane, everyday routine; that life has an inner world, an inner kingdom, a treasure that you are carrying without knowing anything about it.

The master simply provokes you, challenges you.

His silence is a challenge, his words are a challenge. His presence is an invitation.

Those who are alive and those who want to be more alive follow the path; they are very few, unfortunately. Most of the people decide to remain in their eggs. The egg seems to be very protective – who knows what is outside? The egg is a security – who knows, outside may be insecure, unsafe. The master simply gives by his presence the assurance – not by words, but just by his being: "Come out of the egg, come out of your prison whatever is the name of your prison – and you are capable of it."

Nothing is needed to be done from the outside; it is an inner explosion. The gardener does not open the rose petals; the bud opens the petals on its own. Yes, the gardener helps in many other ways, but the central and the essential experience happens from the inside.

I call the man a master who can make you secure in this insecure world, who can give you the courage to come out of your cozy hole, who can give you the insight that you have wings.

I have told you one ancient parable…

A lioness was pregnant and she jumped from one hillock to another hillock and gave birth to a kid, which fell on the ground in a crowd of sheep.

This small lion was brought up by the sheep, although he became a lion. But they became accustomed to him and moreover, he was a vegetarian just as all sheep are. And although sheep or lions don't have mirrors, they felt that something was weird with this sheep…too long, too big, but there was no trouble.

The trouble arose one day when an old lion saw this crowd of sheep going by and, amongst them, a lion, young, strong – and the sheep were not afraid of him!

The old lion could not believe his eyes – it was so absurd! He had to run after him, because the young lion started running with the sheep. He called to him many times, "Stop!"

But the young lion had never thought that he was any-body other than a sheep – perfectly vegetarian, eating grass, having friends, love affairs, girlfriends, enjoying life – why should he stop? And this fellow seems to be dangerous!

But the old lion could not resist the temptation. He fol-lowed and got hold of the young lion and said, "You idiot, have you forgotten that you are a lion?"

The young lion started shivering with fear and he said, "Let me go, my people are going. If they are gone I will be lost. Don't prevent me. Please forgive me; just let me go. They are all going to have a beautiful lunch; just by the side of the river there is such delicious grass. If you want you can come, but don't prevent me."

The old lion said, "You stupid…you come with me. Have you started eating grass?"

The old lion took the young lion forcibly, because he wouldn't budge. He wanted to go to his own people and this fellow was unnecessarily harassing. The old lion took him to the river and told him, "Look into the river and look at my face and your face!"

Nothing was said, nothing was done, and there came a great roar from the young lion. Suddenly, a transformation: he was not a sheep.

But nothing was said. Just a mirror was used, the mirror of a silent river.

The master is only a mirror.

He does not do anything.

He simply allows you to look into the mirror of his eyes, into the mirror of his gestures, into the mirror of his silences, and perhaps there may come the lion's roar.

You may wake up to your reality.

It is so silent and so beautiful, but I would like a little laughter before we experience a deeper silence. Each laughter brings in the wake a deeper silence, a fresher silence....

A young actor has just been hired for his first role in a play being performed on Broadway.

"You have only one line," the director tells him, "but it is an extremely important one. When you hear the sound of guns going off you say, 'Hark! I hear the cannons roar!' Do you understand?"

"Of course," replies the actor confidently, "Hark! I hear the cannons roar! No problem, I've got it already."

The following night the theater is packed and the young actor is striding about backstage repeating over and over, "Hark! I hear the cannons roar."

Then the audience goes quiet as the play begins. The director signals for the young man to go out on the stage and the curtain raises.

Suddenly a loud thundering noise rolls through the theater. The startled actor spins round and shouts, "Shit! What the fuck was that?"

A Texan in England enters a crowded railway carriage. He finds that the only spare seat is occupied by a mean looking dog owned by a fat red-faced woman. He asks politely if the dog can sit on the floor instead of the seat.

"You leave my dog alone!" snaps the woman.

The Texan searches the whole train without finding a seat, so he comes back and throws the dog out of the window.

The woman freaks out. "Are you all going to sit here," she screams at everyone, "and allow an American to treat an English lady like this?"

One man in a bowler hat lowers his *Times* newspaper, "The Americans are all crazy, Madam," he explains. "They hold their fork in the wrong hand, they drive on the wrong side of the road, and now this idiot has gone and thrown the wrong bitch out of the window!"

A Catholic priest in Rome visits a brothel. When he has finished, instead of having to pay he is given ten dollars. The priest rushes off to tell the cardinal about this.

Sure enough, the next day the cardinal goes to the same brothel. When he has finished, instead of having to pay he is given one hundred dollars. The cardinal can't believe his luck. So he runs off to tell Pope the Polack about this incredible deal.

The next night the Polack pope sneaks down to the red-light district and finds the same place. When he has finished they give him a check for a thousand dollars.

"Just a minute," cries the pope, "this is unbelievable! How come you pay the customers here?"

"Well," says the madam, "it is like this. We got a great photograph of the priest in action. We made a great movie out of the cardinal. And right now you are appearing live on satellite television."

A young girl who is getting married asks her mother about the wedding night. Her mother is old-fashioned and tells her, "He will take you to bed, tear off your clothes and then he will lie beside you and then...er, *scare* you! But you will just have to put up with it."

After the first time the young bride looks coyly at her husband. "Darling," she says, "scare me again."

He scares her several times during the night, and when the sun rises the bride shakes her husband and says, "Darling, scare me again."

The man opens his bleary eyes, slowly takes a deep breath and shouts, *"Yaa-boo!"*

Okay...now for two minutes close your eyes, no movement, just be frozen...

Now relax.

Come back.

ALWAYS NOW AND HERE 4

Osho,

Hyakujo and a Wild Duck
When Basho was out walking with Hyakujo he saw a wild duck fly past.
Basho said, "What is it?"
Hyakujo said, "It is a wild duck."
Basho said, "Where is it?"
Hyakujo said, "It has flown away."
Basho at last gave Hyakujo's nose a sharp pinch.
Hyakujo cried out with pain.
Basho said, "There, how can it fly away?"

Setcho says:

The wild duck! What, how and where?
Basho has seen, talked, taught and exhausted
the meaning of mountain clouds and moonlit seas.
But Jo doesn't understand – "has flown away."
Flown away? No, he is brought back!
Say! Say!

Osho,
Basho is said to have been the first Zen master to use
hits, pinches, shouts and pushes to bring a disciple
to the present. But such methods leave themselves
open to abuse and to becoming simply a tradition.
You seem to devise a different method every day
to outsmart us.
You are always at least one step ahead of us!
What do you say?

Maneesha, before Zen master Niskriya takes care of you,
I would like to answer this beautiful anecdote....
Basho has tremendous respect in my heart. He is not only a
mystic, a master, he is also a poet, a painter, a sculptor; he is
a creative phenomenon. Nobody can compare with him as
far as his multidimensional personality is concerned.

Bodhidharma is the greatest peak but he is one-
dimensional. Basho is not that great a peak but he has a

different quality of greatness that is his multidimensionality. Just as Bodhidharma is unique so is Basho. His statements have to be listened to very carefully. He speaks as Basho should speak – he is the very essence of Zen.

If Bodhidharma is the founder then Basho is the flower. He has the fragrance which only a flower can have. That fragrance is manifested in his poetry, in his small statements, in his every gesture. Even in his ordinary talks with people he cannot be other than Basho.

This small anecdote would have been forgotten if Basho were not there. There is nothing new in it but Basho gives it new meaning. There is nothing philosophical or mystical in it, but Basho makes it a mystery. You will have to be very silently aware to see what a great master is....

Bodhidharma is very raw. He smells of the earth when the first rain clouds come – and a beautiful smell out of the earth. Basho is far more refined, perhaps the most refined Zen master up to now. His refinement is in his cultured, meditative spaciousness. Out of that spaciousness many flowers have showered on the world. It does not matter wherever he is and whatever is going on, Basho is going to make it a Zen state of affairs. That uniqueness will not be found again.

Just think of this Hyakujo and a wild duck....

> When Basho was out walking with Hyakujo
> he saw a wild duck flying past.
> Basho said, "What is it?"

Certainly the question is not about the wild duck, because Basho is not blind. Hyakujo is far behind in spiritual growth; he is not yet a master. Not even a perfect disciple. He has some intellectual sophistication, but even he missed it. He missed it because he must have thought that Basho had not seen that it is a wild duck.

Basho is not asking about the wild duck at all. He is not asking about the form but the essence.

"What is it?" He is not asking about the past or the present but that which transcends time.

> Hyakujo said, "It is a wild duck."

Perfectly factual, perfectly right – but not in the eyes of a man like Basho.

> Basho said, "Where is it?"

He gives another chance to Hyakujo and he again misses it.

> Hyakujo said, "It has flown away."
> Basho at last gave Hyakujo's nose a sharp pinch.
> Hyakujo cried out with pain.
> Basho said, "There, how can it fly away?"

So much is implied in this small conversation. First, as we conceive time and as it is in the eyes of the awakened, is not the same.

For us time passes by.

For the awakened one you pass by.

Time is always present. It never goes anywhere.

It is always now and here.

Have you ever met the past? Yes, you have imagined, dreamt about it. But your dreaming about the past is not the past; your imagination is not the reality. Where is the future? – except in your desires and in your longings and in your passions, where is the future? And these longings and desires and greed and ambitions are part of your mind. They are not part of time.

For a man whose desires have disappeared, whose greed is no longer there, do you think there will be even a slight shadow of tomorrow? With the desires and longings going away the future dies, and with the memories and imaginations and the dreams dropping, the past disappears. Then what remains in your hands? You cannot even call it present, because present is possible only if there is something past and something future. In that context the present is the middle, but if the future disappears and the past dies, the present cannot live. The present is also part of your mind.

Your mind is time.

And when times ceases, your mind ceases.

Then you simply are.

You have to understand this background, only then will you be able to see Basho's tremendous insight into things, transforming small experiences into great metaphysical truths.

As he saw the wild duck fly past Basho said, *"What is it?"*

He is not asking about the wild duck, he is asking about *it* – and the *it* contains the whole existence. But obviously anybody who understands only language and knows nothing about that which is beyond language, will agree with Hyakujo.

Hyakujo said, "It is a wild duck."

But he has not understood that Basho would not ask about the wild duck; he can see it himself. He is asking about *it*, another name of existence. *"What is it?"* The wild duck is just an excuse to raise the question: What is existence?

Existence is not a wild duck, although a wild duck is part of existence – but existence is far bigger.

The *it* of Basho contains the totality; the poor wild duck is not even a dewdrop in the ocean. But he gives another chance to Hyakujo to understand that his question is not directed about the wild duck.

Basho said, "Where is it?"

Hyakujo goes on committing the same mistake. That is the nature of mind; it goes on committing the same mistake again and again.

Hyakujo said, "It has flown away."

The simple word *it* in the eyes of Basho contains the whole existence; hence it cannot fly away. Where will it go? It contains all, but poor Hyakujo is still concerned with the wild duck. He cannot understand that a great master like Basho cannot ask such a stupid question and if he is asking, then there must be much more than language contains. He said, "It has flown away" – still he is concerned with the wild duck. Naturally Basho could see that Hyakujo will not understand easily.

Basho at last gave Hyakujo's nose a sharp pinch.
Hyakujo cried out with pain.
Basho said, "There, how can it fly away?"

Existence cannot go anywhere. It is always here. How can it fly away and where? It is everywhere. That small *it* contains the whole.

And Basho is the past master because it began with him that he started hitting his disciples, slapping his disciples, pinching their noses.

Words have failed...what to do? The disciple has to be brought to his senses! Basho gave a sharp pinch to Hyakujo's nose. Hyakujo cried out with pain. Rather than sympathizing or being compassionate,

Basho said, "There..."

Pain brings you here. Pain has a certain quality, the same as pleasure; they bring you here. And a sharp pinch on the nose and Basho asked, "There, when the nose is hurting how can it fly away?"

Setcho comments – his commentaries are becoming better every day:

"The wild duck! What, how, and where?"

In existence everything is formal: today somebody is alive and tomorrow he is gone. Who was he? Where was he and where has he gone? The flower that was dancing in the wind just now is no longer there – all the petals have withered away. From where did that flower come? From where to where has it gone? What was it? Certainly it was not just the petals. It was a certain expression of existence. It was real; it was not a dream.

It came out from nowhere.

It remained in nowhere.

It has gone into nowhere.

Nowhere.

I would suggest to you again to break that word in two:

make it now-here – just a small hyphen. That is the meaning of nowhere. *Now-here* – put together it becomes nowhere, but looked at deeply, *now* and *here* are the realities. Perhaps you cannot see it now. It has entered into its own essence.

Again will come the spring and again will come the flower.

It has been coming again and again and going again and again back into its invisible house – the essence.

> The wild duck! What, how, and where?
> Basho has seen, talked, taught and exhausted the
> meaning of the mountain clouds and moonlit
> seas. But Jo does not understand...
> Flown away?

Setcho is using Hyakujo's everyday name, Jo. Jo does not understand. He sees but he sees only the form. He does not see the formless; otherwise even in the wild duck you will find the same essential soul as you will find within yourself.

The whole existence consists of one soul with millions of formulations – but the content of every form is the same.

> "...has flown away."
> Flown away? No, he is brought back!

By pinching hard on the nose of Hyakujo the wild duck is brought back. Setcho means that if even now he cannot understand that nothing goes anywhere, everything remains here – like the pain. Then the wild duck is brought back.

> Say! Say!

Setcho has the style of repeating his comments with

"Say!" He is commenting in front of disciples. He is asking them, "Say, have you understood it? Is the wild duck back? Say!" In fact it has never gone anywhere, it has been in its essence since eternity and to eternity. For the first time Setcho has made something beautiful, has added something to Basho's statement.

And Maneesha is asking me: "Osho, Basho is said to have been the first Zen master to use hits, pinches, shouts and pushes to bring a disciple to the present. But such methods leave themselves open to abuse and to becoming simply a tradition."

True! That fate has befallen the Zen tradition also; much of it has become dead. Still masters ask, "What is it?" when a wild duck flies over – knowing the whole story, still the noses are pinched – but now it is meaningless. You are right that such methods leave themselves open to abuse and to becoming simply a tradition. Everything outward is going to become a tradition and the moment anything becomes a tradition, it loses meaning.

Is it so easy to understand existence just by giving a pinch to somebody's nose, or shouting, or hitting...? These kinds of strategies can work only once. Basho was very inventive – he never repeated the same strategy again. But even though you are inventive, how many things can you do from the outside? There is a limit.

Maneesha, you are asking, "You seem to devise a different method every day to outsmart us. You are always at least one step ahead of us. What do you say?"

No knowing!

I do not devise. I never know what is going to be my next

word. I allow existence to take me over completely. Hence I have been speaking for thirty-five years but I have never felt that I have repeated anything. Every day everything is fresh; every time it has a new dimension, a new meaning, a new significance; every time a new smell, a new fragrance.

I don't devise, I let the universe devise it. It is not a very great quality; it is sheer laziness. I won't pinch anybody's nose – not because there are noses which do not need to be pinched, but just because I am too lazy. I am so lazy that my physiologist, my physician, Amrito exercises for me. He takes my hand and he tells me, "Don't do anything" – and he exercises my hand…. I said, "Okay."

Now he has imported machines which will exercise for me. I will enjoy seeing my own leg being exercised by a machine. For the first time a buddha is in such a situation!

But as far as invisible hits and shouts are concerned, they happen on their own. I may just look at you, or I may call Master Niskriya – and he was so beautiful. He functioned exactly the way…even Basho would have felt ashamed! When I told him to hit Maneesha hard he kissed her head. No hit can go deeper than a kiss. And when I said to hit anybody with his staff he hit his own head…. Even Basho would have been surprised.

I have my own ways of working, but being lazy I cannot be too physical. I can love you, I can make you laugh, I can make you cry, I can make you wait. That too is not devised, not pre-considered; it just happens.

Just now a fly is moving under my robe – and I am not going to do anything. She has got into trouble by herself – why should I do anything?

Maneesha, I am not even one step ahead of you, I am with you shoulder to shoulder. But I have found more sophisticated, more conscious ways of working on people then Basho himself. I love him; he is my predecessor – but he has to learn much if he comes back.

There is no need to hit somebody's head, because my understanding is that an idiot's head will become even harder. An idiot is not a donkey – that you give a hit of the stick on the donkey's head and you can get the donkey's attention. The ordinary human man lives in such deep unconsciousness that your hit will be misunderstood.

Hyakujo may not understand, but at least he understands that he is missing something. But today, you pinch somebody's nose and you will get a bigger hit on your nose – and the person will say, "I came here to know about God, not to be pinched on my nose…and what have I to do with a wild duck? What kind of nonsense is this…?"

To the contemporary educated man, Zen will appear more mystical than anything. Sometimes not even mystical but pure nonsense, absurd. It was a different climate, a different kind of people – a different air in which Zen was meaningful. Today Basho would be in the Police Commissioner's office: "Why did you hit poor Hyakujo's nose? What kind of master are you?"

But I hit you in my own way…very legal, constitutional, without moving – I have refined much on Basho.

I have told you a story…

An emperor of Japan was very much interested in swordsmanship. Every year he used to give huge awards to the winners. One year it happened that three swordsmen were chosen from different areas of the country. They were all masters and they had no idea what test was ahead. Thousands of other swordsmen were present just to watch, because this was a great occasion to see what a swordsman can do.

The king said, "Get ready," opened a small box – and a fly ran out of the box. The first swordsman cut the fly in the air into two parts. Everybody clapped…the fly was so small, and it was flying!

The second fly was released and the second swordsman cut the fly into three pieces in the air. There was really great clapping, and everybody was waiting for what happens with the third. Now what more can he do? A fly, so small, flying…and he cut it into three pieces in the air. There is not even enough space to make four cuts; just two was too much! The third fly was opened and the third warrior flashed his sword, but the fly went away. So everybody started laughing, that this is stupid, he could not even kill the fly. Even the emperor could not believe why he had been chosen from a province as a great master.

The swordsman said, "Stop laughing! You don't understand. This fly will never reproduce."

Such a fine cut. My flies don't reproduce.

Now a few laughters before we enter into two minutes of silence. These laughters are simply preparations – hence I call them prayers….

One morning at the breakfast table, little Ernie says to his mother, "Mummy, yesterday when you were at work, Daddy took the maid upstairs to the bedroom and…." His mother interrupts him and says, "Ernie, tonight at dinner time I want you to tell this whole story when your father is here."

So that night at dinner his mother says, "Now, Ernie, dear, I want you to repeat what you told me this morning."

"Well," says Ernie, "when you were at work, Daddy took

the maid up to the bedroom and did the same thing you and the milkman did last week."

Gloria is early for her appointment with the optician, so she goes into a shoe store to try on some new shoes.

As the clerk bends over to measure her foot, Gloria, who is very shortsighted, sees his bald head, and thinks it is her bare knee showing. Quickly, she pulls her skirt over it.

Immediately, there is a muffled cry. "Shit!" shouts the clerk, "There goes the electricity again!"

Farmer Hayseed keeps the best bull in the neighborhood and makes money renting its services.

One day, Farmer Hayseed and his son, Ned, leave the bull with young Sam, giving him the instructions to charge ten dollars for every cow that comes to visit it. Sam is sitting in the farmyard when an angry neighbor drives up and demands to see Farmer Hayseed. "He's out, sir," says Sam, "and so is Ned, but I can help you."

"No, you can't," snaps the neighbor, "that Ned has gone and got my daughter pregnant!"

"You're right, sir, you'll have to see Farmer Hayseed," says Sam, "I don't know what he charges for Ned."

Now two minutes of absolute silence.
Just melt into this silence.
Close your eyes…no movement.
Let your whole energy gather within yourself.

Now let go…

Okay, come back.

71

SIGNATURES ON WATER

5

Osho,

Obaku's Partakers of Brewer's Grain
Obaku addressed the assembly and said, "You are all partakers of brewer's grain. If you go on studying Zen like that, you will never finish it. Do you know that in all the land of T'ang there is no Zen teacher?"
Then a monk came forward and said, "But surely there are those who teach disciples and preside over the assemblies. What about that?"
Obaku said, "I do not say that there is no Zen, but that there is no Zen teacher."

Setcho says:

Commanding his way of teaching;
But he made it no point of merit.
Seated majestically over the whole land,
He distinguished the dragon from the snake.
Emperor Taichu once encountered him
And thrice fell into his clutches.

Osho,
Obaku says there is no Zen teacher. It seems to me
therefore that there can be no disciples. So who are
you and who are we?

And the second question:

Obaku seems to be saying that one cannot know
Zen by experiencing one particle of brewer's grain.
But I have heard you say, "Taste one drop of the
ocean, and you know the whole ocean."
Can you please comment?

Maneesha, Zen is the very principle of existence.
Whether there is anyone who teaches it or not,
whether there is anyone who learns it or not, it is there. Zen
is the very heartbeat of existence. It is not dependent on any
teaching, not dependent on any masters, not dependent on

disciples. Masters come and go, disciples come and disappear; Zen remains. Just as it is. It is always just as it is.

I have made my comment.

Now I will take the anecdote:

> Obaku addressed the assembly and said,
> "You are all partakers of brewer's grain. If you go
> on studying Zen like that, you will never finish it.
> Do you know that in all the land of T'ang there is
> no Zen teacher?"
> Then a monk came forward and said, "But surely
> there are those who teach disciples and preside
> over the assemblies. What about that?"
> Obaku said, "I do not say that there is no Zen,
> but that there is no Zen teacher."

I hope things are very simple.

If there is no Catholic church, no pope, there will be no Christianity, because Christianity has nothing to do with existence's essence. If there is no *shankaracharya* and no Hindu monks, existence will just remain the same as it is. Their being or not being does not affect existence. Certainly their doctrines will disappear, their congregations will not be held anymore. Their teachers and their masters and their disciples will not be there. And if these people think Hinduism is dependent on these scriptures, *shankaracharyas*, then certainly there will be no Hinduism either.

Except Zen, no religion has been so intensely clear about its own existential status. The others are only aware about their theologies, their scriptures, their teachers, their masters, their disciples. They are all very superficial – just waves on the ocean. But Zen has never for a single moment identified itself with the waves. It consistently emphasizes, "I am the ocean. Waves come and go; the ocean remains. Many more waves will come and go; it does not affect the ocean in any way."

Obaku was right when he said that there is no Zen. There were many teachers and many followers, but they don't constitute the reality of Zen.

For example, one day I was not and one day I will be again not. The same is true about each of you. But the essence of existence knows no change; it remains. And that essence of existence is called Zen. It is not an ordinary religion like Hinduism, Christianity, Mohammedanism, Buddhism, Jainism, Judaism – I am including even Buddhism – because Zen is the essence; everything else is just commentary. Zen is the experience; everything else is just decoration.

Obaku is right: even though there are Zen masters and there are Zen followers, yet there is no Zen in the sense that these teachings are all superfluous and these teachers are only knowledgeable. They know about Zen, but they have not lived it, they have only learned about it. And when the teachers themselves don't have Zen as a quality of their innermost being, how can they teach anyone? But that does not mean that there is no Zen.

Zen is another name of existence – and then you will be able to understand Obaku very easily.

Setcho says:

> Commanding his way of teaching;
> But he made it no point of merit.
> Seated majestically over the whole land,
> He distinguished the dragon from the snake.

Emperor Taichu once encountered him
And thrice fell into his clutches.

Setcho is appreciating the tremendous insight of Obaku, his clarity of vision in making a distinction between the snake and the dragon, his great capacity to be a master:

Commanding his way of teaching... But he is so humble that *he made it no point of merit.*

Seated majestically over the whole land... He is just a beggar as far as the outside world is concerned, but because of his insight into the very center of existence he is the real emperor. Even a great emperor – *Taichu once encountered him and thrice fell into his clutches.*

We don't know what those clutches were. They are not recorded but they must have been of the same quality. For example, when somebody says, "There is no Zen, although there are Zen teachers and Zen disciples," at the same time he means that these disciples and these teachers make no difference – Zen is.

Zen is rather is-ness. It is in the flowers and it is in the mountains and it is in the clouds. It is in the open sky and it is in the tremendous light of the sun and it is also in the darkness of the night.

It is! Everything else is commentary.

A master is authentic when he knows it as his own being; a master is unauthentic when he does not know it as his own being although he knows all the holy scriptures. He may be a learned scholar and because of his learning he may find disciples, but all are sitting in a wrong boat.

You are asking me, "Osho, Obaku says there is no Zen teacher. It seems to me therefore that there can be no disciples.

So who are we and who are you?"

Obaku's statement does not concern this assembly. At least it does not concern me. He was talking only about his land, centuries before: the land of T'ang, a small province of China. He is not talking about eternity – he cannot talk about me or about you!

I know Zen – not from any scripture. I do not belong to the tradition of Zen; I belong to these clouds. I belong to existence on my own accord. I have found Zen – not through the scriptures. That's why I can say, even in Japan there are only teachers and followers, no Zen. I am almost a stranger to the tradition; but I have found Zen on my own accord. It is my discovery, it is not an inheritance from the tradition, an inheritance from Mahakashyapa, Bodhidharma, Obaku. I don't have anything from these people – I don't owe anything to anybody.

If Obaku were here, then Zen Master Niskriya would have pinched his nose. As his representative, Master Niskriya, pinch Maneesha's nose.

[*Niskriya takes a peacock feather which has been perched on his camera, and tickles Maneesha's nose.*]

Right.... Good!

Maneesha, your second question is: "Obaku seems to be saying that one cannot know Zen by experiencing one particle of brewer's grain. But I have heard you say, 'Taste one drop of the ocean, and you know the whole ocean.' Can you please comment?"

As for my statement, I stand by it, Obaku or no Obaku. I repeat again: If you have tasted a single drop you have tasted the whole ocean. Now you know its saltiness. If you have tasted one moment of silence, you have tasted its blissfulness, its benediction. I don't care what Obaku says. As far as this statement is concerned he is wrong.

I agree with his first statement unconditionally. In the same way I disagree with his second statement, also unconditionally – there is no possibility of compromise. And you can see my point is so clear that Obaku unnecessarily becomes a laughing-stock. He was doing perfectly well, but he went a little too far. He forgot that there would be coming people of greater insight and deeper clarity, who will condemn his second statement.

I am not a man who follows anybody; I am nobody's disciple. I have tasted existence and I have declared that I have known it. Anything that goes against my experience is wrong.

Osho,
The great master Basho was seriously ill.
The chief priest of the temple came to pay his respects.
He asked, "How do you feel these days?"
The master said, "Sun-faced Buddha, moon-faced Buddha."

Setcho says:

Sun-faced Buddha! Moon-faced Buddha!
Compared with them,
How pale the three sovereigns, the five ancestral emperors!
For twenty years I have had fierce struggles,
Descending into the dragon's cave for you.
The hardship defies description.
You clear-eyed monks, don't make light of it.

Osho,
You rarely speak on any hardships you may
experience for us, and I know that some of us tend
to think you are beyond pain or discomfort because
you have the capacity to witness everything.
Some have expressed the idea that your illnesses are
just devices for us.
Could you please comment?

And the second question:

I have heard you say, "This very body, the Buddha,"
and I have also heard you remind us that we are
not the body.
Would you talk about these seemingly opposing
statements?

Maneesha, the clouds have come again....

Basho's statement, *"Sun-faced Buddha, moon-faced Buddha"* looks like a puzzle. It is not. It is simply saying that Buddha is Buddha whether he is sun-faced or moon-faced; Buddha is Buddha whether he is sitting, standing, walking or lying down. In the world of Zen *buddha* simply means your very nature. So whether or not it starts raining, you will be the same, or clouds come thundering – you will be the same. In sickness your consciousness does not become sick; in old age your consciousness does not become old; in death you are not dead. Your buddhahood, your nature, your essence is immortal. This is my comment.

> The great master Basho was seriously ill. The chief
> priest of the temple came to pay his respects.

He asked, "How do you feel these days?"

Just a formal question. But you don't ask formal questions of a man like Basho, because a man like Basho is going to reply something which you had never expected. The master said, *"Sun-faced Buddha, moon-faced Buddha,"* in response to the priest's question, *"How do you feel these days?"* when he was sick.

Basho is saying, "Whether I am sick or healthy, alive or dead, it does not make any difference to my essence. So don't ask such stupid questions." And Basho is certainly one of the most precious men ever born on the earth.

Setcho says:

Sun-faced Buddha! Moon-faced Buddha!
Compared with them,
How pale the three sovereigns, the five ancestral
emperors!
For twenty years I have had fierce struggles,
Descending into the dragon's cave for you.
The hardship defies description.
You clear-eyed monks, don't make light of it.

Setcho has improved a little bit, but a schoolmaster is a schoolmaster. It is really very unlikely for a schoolmaster to become enlightened – at least I have never heard of any such incident when a schoolmaster has become a buddha.

Setcho is trying and because he is just a schoolmaster, knowledgeable, he is going to have a great struggle in finding the truth. The truth is already found, you are just not looking at it. There is no pain, no struggle as far as knowing your being is concerned. But the pain and struggle comes in when you know too much *about* your being, your truth, your enlightenment. All that knowledge becomes mountainous, and then you have to struggle out from your own knowledge.

It is the greatest difficulty to know and to become innocent. Your knowledge prevents you from becoming innocent. There is struggle and there is pain and there is agony, but it has nothing to do with truth; it has something to do with your knowledgeability.

First he is just like a parrot when he repeats: *"Sun-faced Buddha! Moon-faced Buddha!"* There was no need to repeat it, Basho has said it.

For twenty years I have had fierce struggles...

I am absolutely certain that he must have struggled hard. But that struggle is not in finding the truth, that struggle is to get out of your knowledge. The struggle is with the mind, not with the being.

Once you have erased all your knowledge and you have become only no knowing, Zen is in your empty hands. It has always been there, but because of knowledge your eyes were not capable of seeing it. The struggle is with all those theories, theologies, philosophies which are covering your eyes like dust; hence, I don't think that he is making a wrong statement, but he is wrongly understanding the reason for his struggle. Struggle has been there – it is almost as if one is descending into the dragon's cave and then coming out is almost impossible. Knowledge is a far bigger dragon.

Setcho is right that he has fought for twenty years, but he

is not right that he has come out. He still has to fight a little more. He is on the right track, but even the right track is not the goal.

And you are asking, Maneesha: "Osho, you rarely speak on any hardships you may experience for us, and I know that some of us tend to think you are beyond pain or discomfort because you have the capacity to witness everything. Some have expressed the idea that your illnesses are just devices for us. Could you please comment?"

Just bullshit, Maneesha, fresh bullshit...!

I have not struggled at all. I have not suffered in finding the truth. Yes, I have suffered much in transferring it to you. I have taken every pain possible to make you aware of your reality. In a way you are right that my illnesses or my hard-ships are for you, not for me.

Existence has been immensely compassionate, as far as I am concerned. I have not taken even a single step to find it. The reason was that I never got in the clutches of knowl-edgeability; I never became a learned scholar, although there is hardly a single man who has read so much as I have read. But my readings could not pollute my consciousness, they could not corrupt my consciousness; they were just like sig-natures on water.

I have read all the scriptures, but I have not allowed any-thing to be accumulated and fill my inner emptiness. That emptiness is absolutely pure and when I speak, I speak from my own emptiness, from my own purity, from my own inno-cence. Sometimes it coincides, that is another matter, but it coincides only when something matches my experience. Then I can say to Bodhidharma, "I agree – emptiness, no holiness, no knowing."

But when I see a small difference, it does not matter with whom – for example with Joshu, who is considered one of the greatest masters in the Zen tradition, I could not agree, although what he was saying was not absolutely wrong. He was saying, "The way is not difficult." But even this much difference is enough and I can see that he has missed the point. There is no way; hence the question of its being difficult or easy does not arise. You are already there where you want to be.

Maneesha, I have suffered because I love you.

Truth has been very easy to me.

Love has been very difficult.

Truth has been without any struggle.

There was nothing to struggle with – just pure emptiness.

But to transfer that emptiness to you has been a great struggle. For thirty-five years I have been continuously struggling in this way and that way to approach you – somehow to wake you up.

Yes, in that I have suffered much, and I am going to suffer much unless you decide not to hide but to expose yourself, not to remain a seed but start growing. I have suffered because I had to say things which go against traditions, religions, nations. I have made so many enemies in the world that you can call me a great success, a great success in making enemies although I had wanted to be a friend. But this whole business of transferring truth creates enemies easily and friends very rarely.

But I have enjoyed this struggle and will continue to enjoy, whatever pain, whatever agony it brings – perhaps a man like me is destined to be crucified. And that's what the politicians of the whole world and the religious heads of the whole world are trying, but they don't want my blood on their hands. They are trying in every possible way to silence me.

The Attorney General of America, after harassing and torturing and poisoning me said in a press conference, "All that we want is that Osho should not be seen anywhere, not heard by anyone; no news media should report him." That is equivalent to a modern and sophisticated crucifixion. But they have not been able to be successful and they are not going to be successful because nobody has ever loved you so much as I love you. Jesus loved his "father" – you were just sinners to him. Gautam Buddha was afraid even to use the word *love*, because it reminds him of imprisonments, of chains which are created in the name of love.

I am the first in many senses. I love you and I love you so much that I am certain no government, no country, no army, even if they join together.... Now twenty-four countries have joined together in not allowing me to enter their lands – but I have lovers in their lands.

Even my own country has created every kind of hindrance, that I should not be heard by the masses. They don't allow me to move from my home, and they are trying to prevent people from all over the world coming here. But truth is not weak and love is far stronger than all the nuclear weapons.

It may create pain and physical trouble for me, but nobody can put locks on my mouth. They can put chains on my hands – they did; they can put chains on my feet – they did. I am living in a situation which can almost be called house arrest – but I trust in love, that it is going to be victorious.

Even if they kill me my voice will be heard around the earth for as long as there is a single living human being.

Maneesha, your second question is: "I have heard you say,

'This very body, the Buddha,' and I have also heard you remind us that we are not the body. Would you talk about these seemingly opposing statements?"

They are certainly only seemingly opposite. When I said, "This very body, the Buddha," and "This very earth, the paradise," my meaning was, "Don't look anywhere else! Don't look there – look here, look in."

And to make it possible to look in, sometimes I had to say that we are not the body. The first thing is to bring you here. "This body the Buddha," is just to bring you here, and once you are here the second thing is, "Look within; you are not the body but something that the body contains – the emptiness, the nothingness." There is no contradiction; they are two steps of a single process.

Now a few moments to be devoted to laughter. This evening you have been too serious....

The woman was happily showing off her new mink coat to her friend. "It was nice of your husband to buy you that beautiful coat," said the friend.

"He had to," replied the woman. "I caught him kissing the maid."

"How terrible!" exclaimed the friend. "Did you fire her?"

"Not yet," replied the woman, "I still need a new hat."

A young woman went into a bank and asked the clerk for change of a one hundred dollar bill. She handed over the note but the clerk took one look at it and said, "I'm sorry, Miss, but this one hundred dollar bill is a fake."

"Oh, my God!" cried the woman, "I have been raped."

Giles Winterbottom, the farmer, takes his small son,

Jasper, to market one day.

Winterbottom goes to look at the cows and strokes them, pulls their skin and generally fondles them. "Why do you do that?" asks Jasper.

"Well, you see, son," says Winterbottom, "if you want to buy a cow, that is the best way to see if she is healthy."

A few days later, Winterbottom is out in the fields when Jasper comes running up and says, "Dad, there is a traveling salesman in the kitchen, and I think he wants to buy Mom!"

Three old Jewish mothers meet at a party in New York.

"There is nobody like my son," says the first. "Every winter he buys me a new fur coat."

"That's nothing," gloats the second. "*My* son takes me to the best travel agent in the town every year and arranges the summer vacation of my choice."

"That's all rubbish!" laughs the third. "My son goes to the most expensive psychiatrist in the whole world and all he does is talk about me!"

Now two minutes of absolute silence.

Close your eyes, gather your energy in.

Now relax...

Now, come back.

PERFECT THE CIRCLE, PURE THE SOUND   6

Osho,

Chinso Shosu Comes to Visit Shifuku
Chinso came to see Shifuku. Shifuku drew a circle in the air.
Chinso said, "I have no object in coming here. Why do
you bother to draw a circle?"
Shifuku closed the door of his room.

Setcho says:

Perfect the circle, pure the sound,
Bright and abundant the encircling jade,
Loaded on horses and mules.

Loaded on board the iron boats,
Given to those who know
The peace and freedom of land and sea.

He put down the tackle to fish the turtle.
Setcho comments here:
"Monks throughout the world can't jump out of it."

Osho,
I know you will have me hit or pinched if I've got it
wrong, but it seems to me that in the same situation
as Shifuku you might have drawn a spiral instead.

The second question:

I recall hearing you say recently that dialogue
between an enlightened and an unenlightened
person is not possible, and between two
enlightened people, not necessary. Zen seems
to be an existential dialogue – the ultimate form of
communication, whether those on either end of the
exchange are enlightened or not.
Would you comment?

The third question:

Some Zen anecdotes are about interchanges

between two masters, two enlightened beings. I
have heard that this was called doing Dharma Battle.
What was the point of those exchanges, or were
they just for the joy of the game?

And the last question:

It seems that the very spirit of Zen is pervading
these evenings with you – through your words,
your gestures, your silences, and our response of
silence or laughter, let-go or Yaa-Hoo!
When communication is total, it feels as if the communicators disappear. Thus when communication
really happens there is no one left to communicate!
Could you please comment?

Maneesha, the dialogue between two enlightened persons is just playfulness. It does not matter whether
they sit silently together or speak. In that space, words or no
words are equivalent.

There is nothing to say and nothing to hide but only
a sharing, a sharing of the joy, a sharing of the awakening, a
sharing of the blissfulness, a sharing of their ecstasy. The
awakened one becomes just a child collecting seashells on the
sea beach, or running after butterflies, or trying to catch
the rainbows.

In fact, dialogue in words is not possible. They can play
with words, but the real dialogue happens in their silences.
And particularly the Zen masters are immensely inventive of
new ways how to play, so that it does not disturb the silence
but on the contrary, enhances it, deepens it, makes it more
sweet, more alive, more dancing.

The silence between two enlightened ones is the greatest poetry – poetry without words, the greatest music – music without sounds. But when there were encounters between Zen masters, they really enjoyed it, playing all kinds of tricks on each other. They are rascal saints.

That is my comment.

> Chinso came to see Shifuku.
> Shifuku drew a circle in the air.

Signifying that here everything is as complete as a circle. The circle is the only thing that cannot be incomplete. If it is incomplete, it is not a circle – it may be anything. A circle by intrinsic necessity has to be complete. *Shifuku drew a circle in the air* to indicate two things: Here everything is complete. Why have you unnecessarily come here? Because the completion cannot speak. It has gone far beyond language. Completion means absolute silence. Why have you come here? That is the question inherent in the circle drawn in the air.

And the second thing: a circle in the air signifies that everything in this world, in this existence, is nothing but circles in the air; don't pay too much attention to it. It is all made of the stuff dreams are made of. Even dreams have some stuff, but a circle in the air is just emptiness. Shifuku has explained his situation so beautifully, so poetically and so truthfully that he cannot be transcended.

> Chinso said, "I have no object in coming here.
> Why do you bother to draw a circle?"

Both are enlightened persons, so naturally Chinso says, *"Why do you bother to draw a circle?"* "Do you think I don't understand? Do you think I cannot draw these circles in the air? And from where have you got the idea that I have come for any special object to be with you?" He is saying, "Is it not possible just to be together out of love, out of playfulness; has it always to be business? Can't it be simply meeting with no object, no goal?"

Both are tremendously insightful, but Chinso is left behind by Shifuku.

Shifuku closed the door of his room.

It is not unwelcoming. He is saying, "If there is no object in coming, if there is nothing to say, nothing to listen to, I am not interested in playing. I have left those childhood toys far behind."

His closing the door is simply mystifying. He is not a man without compassion and he is not a man who has no respect for others — but he has to close the door. In his clarity perhaps Chinso has had some glimpses, but he is still not fully awakened. This closing of the door may help.

Setcho says:

Perfect the circle, pure the sound,
Bright and abundant the encircling jade,
Loaded on horses and mules,
Loaded on board the iron boats,
Given to those who know
The peace and freedom of land and sea.

Setcho is Setcho. Where he has no business, there too he tries to make some commentary....

Now his whole comment is absurd. Just a pure silence would have been enough, but he has taken it upon himself – being a schoolmaster – that he has to explain everything. He himself does not understand and he is trying to explain it to others. This is not only Setcho's situation, this is the situation of millions of people who know nothing, but who go on giving advice to everybody.

It is said that advice is the only thing that is given freely and nobody takes it. A man of real wisdom does not open his mouth unless invited, but the ignorant enjoys advising very much; his understanding is that the more he gives advice the more people will think he is a man of wisdom. But you can fool only those who are already foolish....

Setcho goes on saying:

> He put down the tackle to fish the turtle.
> Setcho comments here:
> "Monks throughout the world can't jump out of it."

In his whole commentary only this statement is significant. How can you jump out of a circle drawn in the air? But in fact, there is no need to jump out of it. The need is to jump in – that is my reply to Setcho.

Maneesha, you have asked a few questions....

First: "Osho, I know you will have me hit or pinched if I have got it wrong, but it seems to me that in the same situation as Shifuku you might have drawn a spiral instead."

You are right, Maneesha: existence is not a circle but a spiral. A circle is static, dead; a spiral goes on growing, goes on becoming bigger. Now the scientists can measure fourteen billion light-years and they say that a tremendous thing is happening that far away. It must affect us too. Galaxies upon galaxies are running in one direction. We cannot see toward what goal they are running, or if there is any goal – or if the running itself is the goal.... But as far as we can see with our instruments, the whole of existence is running fast. Nothing is static; everything is growing bigger and bigger and bigger.

So you are right, I would not have drawn a circle, because I believe in evolution. I believe in no end to evolution, open-ended evolution – evolution for always. I don't believe in any full point, not even in a comma.

But on the other point you are wrong. You say, "I know you will have me hit or pinched if I've got it wrong...." There you are wrong.

Wrong or right, Master Niskriya, hit! That's good.

[*Niskriya takes his feather and tickles her nose.*]

That's very fine.

Your second question: "I recall hearing you say recently that dialogue between an enlightened and an unenlightened person is not possible, and between two enlightened people, not necessary. Zen seems to be an existential dialogue – the ultimate form of communication, whether those on either end of the exchange are enlightened or not. Would you comment?"

Your question is again mixed. Half of it is right: Zen is an existential dialogue, but not between the enlightened and the unenlightened – that is an impossibility. One who knows and one who does not know cannot have any kind of communication. It is just like you are fast asleep and somebody else is talking to you. Now, between the asleep and the awakened, what kind of dialogue...?

But between two awakened, two enlightened persons, dialogue – although unnecessary – is possible. Unnecessary, because they have nothing to convey to each other; they both know it. But Zen is a very youthful, joyous approach to reality; they go on playing with each other. Their play is a joy for those who can understand even the playfulness. They may not understand the meaning of it....

Your idea that it happens whether those on either end of the exchange are enlightened or not, is not right. The enlightened and the unenlightened cannot even play – there is no possibility of communication. When both are enlightened, all possibilities of communication open, but there is nothing to communicate; hence the drama of dialogue.

Your third question is: "Some Zen anecdotes are about interchanges between two masters, two enlightened beings. I have heard that this was called doing Dharma Battle. What was the point of those exchanges, or were they just for the joy of the game?"

Maneesha, Dharma Battle in Pali or Dharma Battle in Sanskrit has a certain subtle purpose. If you see two enlightened persons engaged in a playful dialogue one never knows: the seer within you may become suddenly aware of something more that is not available to our ordinary eyes.

These Dharma Battles are for the growth of insight in disciples. There is nothing to say and there is nothing to be heard, but those who cannot understand silence...something has to be done for them. Something – however far-fetched – but something has to be done. That something is Dharma Battle.

Two enlightened masters meet, poke and pinch each other, raise questions which they know are absurd, give answers which they know have no validity…. But in their Dharma Battle the disciples who are the watchers may become aware of something subtle that is not clear in the words.

For example, one Zen master is making a circle in the air…. You cannot forget that gesture; you will have to figure out what it means. Another enlightened man has come to see him and he closes the door. The very situation is such that you are bound to be engaged, for the first time thinking about something: What do these fellows mean? Drawing a circle in the air, closing the door on the face of the guest…?

It can't just be what it appears to be; it must be something else. It can trigger off an inquiry in the disciple. That is the purposeless purpose.

Your fourth question, Maneesha: "It seems that the very spirit of Zen is pervading these evenings with you – through your words, your gestures, your silences, and our response of silence or laughter, let-go or Yaa-hoo!

"When communication is total it feels as if the communicators disappear. Thus when communication really happens there is no one left to communicate! Could you please comment?"

Niskriya, could you please act again on my behalf?

[*Niskriya touches Maneesha's head with his feather.*]

It is true, Maneesha, these evenings have been very special and those who are present are very fortunate. The silences, the laughter, my eyes and your eyes meeting, my hands being understood…and we have created a golden age which has disappeared from the world. We have brought back the times of Mahakashyapa, Bodhidharma…. This assembly would have made any enlightened person rejoice.

It is true that when communication happens, the communicators disappear – you can feel it immediately. Here you are as if one consciousness, undivided. In your silence you are one, in your laughter you are one. This oneness is the door to the ultimate awakening of your consciousness.

We have been one in silence, let us also be one in our laughter. To me a silence that cannot laugh is dead and a laughter that has no silence in it is superficial. When silence and laughter meet they create a dance, and our effort here is to join in this cosmic dance.

Just relax into the whole...

Don't keep yourself as a spectator.

Don't remain separate....

Gloria and Barbara are chatting together. "What has become of that nice man you started going out with?"

"Oh, I gave him the push!" replies Barbara. "He was no gentleman."

"Whatever happened?" asks Gloria.

"Well," replies Barbara, "no sooner were we alone on the sofa at my place, than he put his hand on my thigh."

"Well," says Gloria, "at least that shows he is interested."

"It might do," replies Barbara, "but I was brought up properly, and I am not going to tolerate that. Everybody knows that with a *real* gentleman, it is always *tits* first!"

Myrtle MacTavish is being treated by her doctor for sore knees. The treatment makes no improvement and Doctor Dingle is puzzled.

"Something is rubbing the skin off your knees as fast as it heals," he says. "Is it praying?"

"No, Doctor," replies Myrtle, "it is my husband. He

insists on having sex on the floor, doggie style."

Doctor Dingle sends for her husband and tells him, "You know, there are plenty of other positions for sex."

"No, Doc, there aren't," replies the man, "not if you both want to watch television."

A young man sitting at a bar sees an attractive girl and offers to buy her a drink.

"Did you say a motel?" asks the girl in a loud voice.

The man is extremely embarrassed and assures her that he only wants to buy her a drink.

"You want to take me to a motel?" she screams.

Everyone turns to look at the young man, and even the bartender tells him to behave himself. He is so embarrassed that he goes and sits at a corner table.

A short while later the girl comes over to him.

"I must apologize," she says. "I am sorry to embarrass you so much, because you see, I am a psychology student and I wanted to take note of your reactions for my psychology thesis."

"What?" shouts the man. "You must be joking! Twenty dollars!"

Now let our laughter become silence.
For two minutes no movement, closed eyes, contain
all your energy inward.

Now relax...

Okay, come back.

JUST BE

7

Osho,

Chimon's Lotus Flower
A monk asked, "What will the lotus flower be when it has not yet come out of the water?"
Chimon said, "The lotus flower."
The monk asked Chimon, "What about when it is out of the water?"
Chimon said, "The lotus leaves."

Setcho says:

The lotus leaves! The lotus flower!
He is so kind to tell you of them!
The flower coming out of the water –
What difference, before or after?
If you wander about, now north of the river,
now south of the lake,
Questioning Master Wang and the like,
As one doubt is settled others will arise,
And you will puzzle over question after question.

Osho,
Isn't the lotus flower a lotus flower at its
conception, when it is floating in the pond,
and when it is plucked from the pond?

And:

I have heard you tell us time and again that the
realization of our enlightenment is inevitable –
whether it be this minute, tomorrow, or the next
life around.
Would you talk about where the individual's
responsibility lies for what is going to happen
anyway?

And the third question:

What are the prerequisites for being a disciple?

Maneesha...

What is, is.
It is never different.
Its forms differ but its being remains the same.
To live in the forms is to live in illusions.
To see the being is to transcend the world.
Only seeing is needed.
What you are going to see is already there – has been there since eternity...waiting and waiting and waiting....
This is my comment.

Chimon is one of the greatest masters.

> A monk asked Chimon, "What will the lotus flower
> be when it has not yet come out of the water?"
> Chimon said, "The lotus flower."
> The monk asked, "What about when it is out of
> the water?"
> Chimon said, "The lotus leaves."

There ends the dialogue – it seems the monk has understood.

Chimon has made an existential statement. Even in the seed the lotus flower is a lotus flower. You cannot see it but its being does not depend on your seeing. If it was dependent on your seeing, then certainly the seed cannot be called the lotus flower, it will be a lotus flower only when floating on the water with open leaves, dancing in the sun.

But that which floats on the water, if it is not hidden in the seed, from where can it come? In the seed it was invisible to our eyes. Our eyes have their limitations; our eyes could see it only when it started floating on the water. That is our limitation; it is not a change as far as the lotus flower is concerned.

Just a few days ago, in France a woman gave birth to a child. The doctors could not believe it; they were expecting something strange, but not what actually happened. The woman was a scientist working in an atomic plant...for nine months the child was exposed to radiation. The doctors were aware that something strange was going to happen, and something strange happened: the child was born with X-ray eyes; the child could see through your skin into your skeleton. That makes an important discovery, that eyes can be changed into X-ray mechanisms. Then you can see things which are hidden, then you can see things which are not available to other people's eyes.

In the Soviet Union a certain photographer has developed a new kind of photography, Kirlian – that is his name – using very sensitive films. He can see the lotus flower in the seed. You give him the seed and his camera will give you the photograph of a lotus flower. Wait for six months, and then, when the lotus flower comes within the limits of visibility, you will be surprised. The photograph will be exactly the same as the actual lotus flower. The sensitive film, the sensitive lenses, could see what we are not able to see.

It simply means that our senses have a limitation, but existence has no limitations.

If we could see the whole with all its implications, then the child will also show you the young man he is going to be, the old man that he is going to be...the sicknesses, the health, the intelligence, the death. In a single flash you will be able to see the whole biography of the child.

But perhaps it is good that we cannot see that much. To see that much will be very confusing. A man is passing and you see a child passing, a young man passing, an old man passing – and he is dead and on the funeral pyre. It will be so quick that you will not be able to decide what is happening. In a single split moment everything has happened. Life will become impossible.

But meditation gives a clarity and a different way of seeing. The lotus flower is a lotus flower in all its forms: when it is a seed, when it is a bud, when it is a flower.

And again it will disappear from your vision.

The petals will go away.

There will be no lotus flower.

Again the pond is empty as it was before.

The lotus flower happened just like a small dream – a glimpse.

That's what Bodhidharma insisted: Emptiness.

Everything comes out of it and everything returns to it, and there is nothing holy because there is nothing unholy. This is not knowledge, conceptual knowledge, this is existential experience; hence, Bodhidharma could say, "No knowing." He is describing himself as no knowing. He is saying, "I am just a mirror. Things come before me, reflect within me, disappear. I remain as empty as ever" – just like the mirror.

Have you ever thought that the mirror is empty, utterly empty? It is because of its emptiness that it is possible for it to reflect anything that comes in front of it. The moment the thing has gone out of the area of the mirror, the mirror is again empty; in fact, even when it was reflecting there was no doing on its part. It is just the nature of the mirror to reflect. It was simply functioning in its nature.

Chimon's statement is absolute, unconditional, categorical.

It contains the whole philosophy of existence: No beginning, no end, everything just is.

Just listen to the clouds.... A moment before they were not there and suddenly they are – and they are going. But existentially they are always: sometimes manifest, sometimes unmanifest.

Chimon needs no commentary, but Setcho is bound to comment. He says:

> The lotus leaves! The lotus flower!
> He is so kind to tell you of them!

It is not a question of kindness. What else can he say? He is simply reflecting the truth. Do you think when a mirror reflects your face it is kind, compassionate? It is simply its nature, the nature of enlightenment that it becomes reflective of reality.

But Setcho – as I have told you – is a schoolmaster! Once in a while, perhaps accidentally, he makes some good statement, but otherwise he is a knowledgeable, confused man.

> The flower coming out of the water –
> What difference, before or after?
> If you wander about, now north of the river,
> now south of the lake,
> Questioning Master Wang and the like.
> As one doubt is settled others will arise,
> And you will puzzle over question after question.

Without any reason or rhyme, he is bringing in Master Wang and criticizing him. Wang is a different type of master, certainly, but he is not wrong, he is simply different. He has a more philosophical approach to reality. His experience is that of a mystic, but his expression is that of a philosopher.

But this is no time or place to bring his name. This shows that Setcho cannot see the difference between the personalities of the masters. Chimon is a simple man; he simply says what he sees. Wang is a different kind of master. He also says what he sees, but he is far more sophisticated. He brings more conceptual knowledge to express his experience.

Setcho, although making the commentary, does not know what he is saying. Chimon and Wang are two forms of the same lotus: one is a simple villager, the other is very cultured, sophisticated, a philosopher.

If he cannot understand this, how can he understand: *The lotus leaves! The lotus flower!...The flower coming out of the water – What difference, before or after?* What he is saying is true, but he is saying it without knowing, without understanding its implications. And he exposes himself immediately the moment he starts criticizing Master Wang. What difference whether you say it directly or in a roundabout way? The lotus flower is the lotus flower – seen by a simple man or by a philosopher, seen by a simple villager or by a great painter. Certainly their visions will be different, but what they are seeing is the same lotus flower.

Maneesha, you are asking: "Osho, isn't the lotus flower a lotus flower at its conception, when it is floating in the pond and when it is plucked from the pond"

No, Maneesha, a lotus flower is a lotus flower. Whether you see it or not, whether it is in the seed or floating in the water, it is simply the change of the form. But the essence – and we are calling the lotus flower the essence – is not its particular expression.

You are asleep or you are awake…. Spiritually you are still asleep; perhaps one day you will become spiritually awake too. But all the time it is you – awake or asleep, enlightened or unenlightened. The lotus flower is the lotus flower.

Your second question is: "I have heard you tell us time and again that the realization of our enlightenment is inevitable – whether it be this minute, tomorrow, or the next life around. Would you talk about where the individual's responsibility lies for what is going to happen anyway?"

There is no question of the individual's responsibility. The very idea of individual responsibility will postpone what is going to happen anyway. Why has it not happened up to now? Why is it not happening? If it is inevitable you don't have to do anything: it is going to happen. All that you can think of doing is to wait with love, trust – in silence – and the guest will come. You cannot manage the guest to come; you can only be just an available host: no responsibility, just a pure awaiting….

That's why I have not given you any discipline, I have not asked you to do this or that. I have only wanted you to understand the fact that enlightenment is your nature, so there is no need to run here and there trying to find where enlightenment is.

Just relax in your silence, in your laughter.

Let your laughter and silence become one.

The moment laughter and silence become one, you create a great alchemical change within you. A dance arises in every fiber of your being, a light, a bliss, a certainty that you have come home.

The word *responsibility* is a little heavy. And whenever people tell you "this is your responsibility" they make you feel guilty, they make you feel burdened. I cannot do that. I want you to be absolutely unburdened, unloaded.

Just *be*.

Don't run after being, because you are already there, where any Buddha has reached. It was his choice to go on a long route of six years and then to come home, tired. And because he was tired he relaxed. He could have relaxed without doing all that he had been doing. The day he relaxed, he became enlightened.

It is only a question of recognition, not responsibility. Even this moment there is no one here who is not a buddha, no one here who is not a lotus flower. Yes, a few are asleep, a few are in the seed, a few are floating in the water, but it does not make any difference. Don't make it hardship; let it remain as light as possible.

My contribution to the religious growth of humanity is that you don't have to do anything, you have just to be at your center – utterly relaxed, no desire, no longing, nowhere to go. Just being here – and the explosion, and the lotus flower.

Your third question, Maneesha: "What are the prerequisites for being a disciple?"

None at all.

An open heart, a loving heart, a deep trust in oneself and nothing else is needed. You don't have to surrender to some master, you don't have to worship some God, you don't have to do some prayer to some hypothetical deity. You don't have to go to manmade temples and churches to find that which is hidden within you.

A disciple is the seed of a master. The disciple is also a lotus flower, it is just that you are looking somewhere else and not within yourself.

Let us laugh a little.... The silence should not become heavy, it should not have weight. Unless your silence learns to dance it becomes a heavy weight.

A flea rushes into the pub just before closing time, orders three large whiskeys, drinks them straight down, rushes out into the street, leaps high into the air and falls flat on his face.

The flea picks himself up shakily and looks all around, "Damn it," he says, "someone has moved my dog!"

Hannibal Hayne is in Doctor Feelgood's office for his annual checkup.

"You won't live out the week," says the doctor, "if you don't stop running around after women."

"But Doc, there is nothing the matter with me," says Hannibal, pounding his chest with his fist, "I am in great physical shape."

"Yes, I know," replies Doctor Feelgood, "but one of the women is my wife."

Fagin Finkelstein, the lawyer, is engaged to defend a man in court on a rape charge. A huge black woman is testifying that she woke up one morning to discover that she had been raped and that the accused was lying beside her.

"Now, madam, it is very hard to take your story seriously," sniggers Fagin. "Suppose, for instance, you had woken in the morning and found *me* lying beside you. What would you think?"

The woman looks Fagin up and down slowly and then remarks, "I would think I had a miscarriage."

Pitkin, the absent-minded professor and his family are

moving house. Mrs. Pitkin knows how forgetful her husband can be and writes the new address on several pieces of paper, putting one in each pocket of the professor's clothes.

Somehow during the day Professor Pitkin manages to write notes on each piece of paper and then give them away to his students.

In the evening when he drives to the old house, he remembers that he has moved, but has no idea where to. Then he sees some children playing in the street and walks over to them.

"Hey, little girl," he calls out, "Can you tell me where the Pitkins have moved to?"

"Sure," replies the girl. "It is just around the corner and three houses along – Daddy!"

Now, two minutes for absolute silence.
Be still, no moving.
Gather your energy inside just as a lotus flower closes
its petals.

Now, relax...

Okay, come back.

THE VOICE OF THE RAINDROPS   8

Osho,

Kyosei's Voice of the Raindrops
Kyosei asked a monk, "What is the noise outside?"
The monk said, "That is the voice of the raindrops."
Kyosei said, "Men's thinking is topsy-turvy. Deluded by their own selves, they pursue things."
The monk asked, "What about yourself?"
Kyosei said, "I was near it but am not deluded."
The monk asked, "What do you mean by 'near it but not deluded'?"
Kyosei said, "To say it in the sphere of realization may be easy, but to say it in the sphere of transcendence is difficult."

Setcho put it like this:

The empty hall resounds with the voice of the raindrops.
Even a master fails to answer.
If you say you have turned the current,
You have no true understanding.
Understanding? No understanding?
Misty with rain, the northern and southern mountains.

Osho,
I wish I could tell Setcho that in our assembly, "An empty hall resounding with the voice of raindrops," is our master's answer.

And question two:

You have never failed to answer – or at least whenever I have listened for it, I have always heard a response. What is your comment?

And question three:

When one's own voice becomes the voice of the raindrops – is that your constant milieu?

Maneesha, the sound of raindrops is not there today but the sound of the bamboos is filling the whole being of this assembly. It is the same.

It does not matter whether it is the sound of running water or the crackling of bamboos – if you are silent, you are not; only the sound of the bamboos fills the whole sphere.

What else remains? – just a pure awareness.

You cannot identify this awareness with yourself. It is transcendental to you, it is higher than you, it is bigger than you. It is your intrinsic treasure, but the lotus is still in the seed.

This anecdote very beautifully makes the point, never mentioning the word *awareness*. There are reasons not to mention the word. Because of your old habit of the mind, you immediately grab on to anything – awareness, consciousness, witnessing – and immediately you think, "It is me."

> Kyosei asked a monk, "What is the noise outside?"
> The monk said, "That is the voice of the raindrops."
> Kyosei said, "Men's thinking is topsy-turvy. Deluded by their own selves, they pursue things."
> The monk asked, "What about yourself?"
> Kyosei said, "I was near it but am not deluded."
> The monk asked, "What do you mean by 'near it but not deluded'?"
> Kyosei said, "To say it in the sphere of realization may be easy, but to say it in the sphere of transcendence is difficult."

Ordinarily, if you had come across such an anecdote, you would have passed without paying any attention to its meaning and significance. Who cares what is the noise outside? It may be the raindrops, it may be birds singing, it may be bamboos dancing in the wind.

Kyosei is asking, *"What is the noise outside?"* The question has a great implication. You can answer it if you are inside, otherwise who will answer? "What is the noise outside?" can be answered only by a consciousness within. If you are asleep you cannot answer, "What is the noise outside?" If you are unconscious you cannot answer, "What is the noise outside?"

Kyosei is not really interested in the noise outside, he is interested in: "Are you in? Are you aware?" But the monk missed, because he said, *"That is the voice of the raindrops."*

Kyosei is not asking anything about the objective world, the outside world, although the question appears to be so. If the monk had remained silent, allowing the raindrops to create the sound, or the bamboos....

In this moment, except your silence there is no answer. Silence is the answer. The moment you speak even a single word you have missed: *Kyosei said, "Men's thinking is topsy-turvy. Deluded by their own selves, they pursue things."* Kyosei has not taken note, has not paid attention to the monk's answer that it is the voice of the raindrops. Instead he says, "Men's thinking is topsy-turvy." In this small sentence there is hidden a great secret. Perhaps you may not have ever thought about *you*.

If in this hall there were nobody, do you think the bamboos would still be making noise? Without you, for whom will they make the noise? Noise needs somebody to hear it. If there is nobody to hear it, there is no noise. When everybody has gone in the middle of the night, the bamboos may try hard, but they cannot make the noise because there are no ears! But even if there are ears and the mind is full of thoughts, the poor bamboos will not be heard.

You are needed and you are needed in such a way as if you

are not. Your presence is needed; your personality is not needed. *You* are needed – your mind is not needed. Then there is a simple awareness of the rain falling, or the water running, or the wind passing through the pine trees, or the bamboos saying *Upanishads*....

Do you see, in this silence the clouds fill you with immense gratitude; their joy becomes contagious. The fresh breeze comes, touches you and gives a dance to every fiber of your being.

...And the rain has come.

The bamboos crying for it has not been in vain.

Kyosei wanted *you*; his audience the monk was a poor fellow. He could not understand that it is not the rain and its sound that is important; what is important is your awareness. The monk must have been a little stupid. Instead of understanding what Kyosei has said, that your mind is topsy-turvy, he asked, *"What about yourself?"*

Kyosei was certainly compassionate...otherwise it was time to get rid of the monk. He said, *"I was near it but I am not deluded."*

This is a very subtle answer. He is not saying, "I am aware of it." He is saying, "I am very close to awareness, but I am not deluded; I will not say that I am aware"...because the moment you make static statements you start going wrong. Life is a continuous flow; so is awareness, so is the whole existence. You cannot use the word, which makes it static – and language is very dead; it consists only of dead words.

Hence Kyosei said, "I was near it, I was just coming closer, but I was not identified even with my awareness. I would not say that I was aware. I can only say, slowly I was becoming aware of it."

It is a delicate point, because Gautam Buddha – who is

the source of Zen Buddhism – does not believe that even for a single moment anything is unchanging.

A man asked Gautam Buddha a question one day – just in the morning – and Buddha answered. But the man could not understand the answer, so in the evening he asked again. Buddha answered again. The man was amazed, because in the morning it had been something else.

Buddha said, "Of course. It was morning and now it is evening, the sun is setting. I am flowing with life and with my flowing my answers will be changing. I cannot give you a static dogma."

Any authentic man of experience is never dogmatic. He cannot say that it is absolutely so because even while you are saying it, it may have changed.

One day you will become old – it is difficult to say which will be the day, but certainly it must be one of the seven days. A few people become old on Monday, a few people choose Sunday…but everybody at some point of time becomes old.

But remember, you cannot simply jump from youth to old age. It is not possible that on Sunday you are young, and early in the morning on Monday you find you have become old. You are becoming old every moment; every moment the flow of life is taking you toward old age, toward death, and toward beyond-death.

How can we say what is the truth?

Kyosei said, "I was near it." In fact one is always coming closer and closer and closer. One never really comes, one goes on coming like waves of the ocean. One wave upon another wave, they go on coming. And they have been coming for millions of years and they have not reached anywhere; they still go on coming. Their life span is not very big, only a few million years; your life span is infinite, from eternity to eternity you are coming, moment to moment, closer and closer.

And this is the beauty of life, that you are always coming closer to it, but you never come to a full stop; the full stop will really mean death. What will you do then?

Have you ever thought about it? If you become realized, enlightened, awakened, then…back to the kitchen, looking into the refrigerator! What are you going to do after that?

Enlightenment cannot be the full point. Buddha had no possibility to open a refrigerator, but in his own old-fashioned way, he immediately starts with his begging bowl – that is not different, just an old version. After enlightenment comes the begging bowl, and he is moving on from house to house.

Today it will be different. You become enlightened. You wait a few minutes in Buddha Hall, waiting and thinking, What to do now? And then you start moving toward the restaurant – in a queue…enlightened people!

It is so hilarious but so human. What else to do?

A few go a little earlier to be just in the front of the line; a few are more patient, a few stay even for hours…but it does not matter, finally you have to go to the restaurant.

Life goes on whether you are enlightened or not.

Kyosei says, "I was near it, very near it. I had almost found it but I will not be deluded, I will not be identified. I will not say, 'I have found it.' I will only say, 'Almost.'"

It was Gautam Buddha's common habit to start his sentences with "Perhaps." Certainty is only for the idiots. For those who even come close to truth everything becomes flexible, everything becomes "Perhaps…." *The monk asked, "What do you mean by 'near it but not deluded'?" Kyosei said, "To say it in the sphere of realization may be easy, but to say it in the sphere of transcendence is difficult."*

He says, "It may be easy if you are ready to commit a small linguistic mistake. You can say, 'I have attained,' but in the true world of transformation it is difficult. You can only say, 'I have come very close, almost to the point of declaring,' but there one stops."

And it is better from there to go to the restaurant. Rather than first becoming enlightened and then going to the restaurant...it doesn't look right...!

Setcho put it like this:

The empty hall resounds with the voice
of the raindrops,
Even a master fails to answer.
If you say you have turned the current,
You have no true understanding.
Understanding? No understanding?
Misty with rain, the northern and southern
mountains.

Once in a while this schoolmaster, Setcho, also manages to say some significant things.

The empty hall... This hall can be said to be empty if you are silent. It is not your being here that disturbs its emptiness, it is your chattering mind that disturbs its emptiness. If the mind is at ease then it resounds only with the raindrops or the bamboos or the clouds, but the hall is empty: *"The empty hall resounds with the voice of the raindrops. Even a master fails to answer."*

There are questions which can be answered only by not answering. If somebody asks you, "Have you stopped beating your wife?" you will be shocked for a moment because whatever you say will have some implications. If you say, "Yes, I have stopped," that means you have been beating. If you say "No" that means you are still beating.

One very intelligent philosopher and logician, seeing such situations has developed a word *po*. When you cannot say yes and you cannot say no, say po. *Po* means nothing; *po* means it is not answerable. Po is a new contribution to language. Perhaps rather than po you would like – because it reminds you about the pope and Poland...You can use Yaa-Hoo! That is specially yours.

And there are idiots who have started writing articles against Yaa-Hoo – quoting Sushrut, an ancient man of medicine – talking about ayurveda, just creating jargon, that this word, *Yaa-Hoo* will destroy people's minds, will break down their nervous systems.

I have told my doctors – we have many experts in everything – to give good hits to these two idiots. In the first place neither has Sushrut mentioned "Yaa-Hoo" anywhere nor is it mentioned in any ayurvedic scripture. They are just throwing big names around.

The reality is that scientific research in the Soviet Union and in America both support that laughing and crying are immensely healthy, healing and refreshing processes. On scientific grounds from many experiments it has been found that if you start laughing, your whole being vibrates with healing energy. It is still a mystery why it happens, but the same happens with crying.

Everybody knows from his own experience that after laughter, good laughter, a belly laughter, you almost feel that you have taken an ice-cold shower. A peace, a silence, a freshness...

The same is true about crying, but very few people know

the secret of crying because it is more repressed than laughter.

Both these people who have written articles – and just today I have seen them – are ayurvedic physicians. It is absolutely certain that they understand that if by laughter people can heal themselves, if by crying people can heal themselves, it goes against their profession. It is not a coincidence that only two *vaidyas*, ayurvedic physicians, should write the article – and without any experimentation. They should come here and participate in the groups.

They must have been afraid that this would be my response, so in their article they say, "We would like to be observers, but not participants."

If you are just an observer and don't take the medicine yourself, how are you going to know what the medicine does? If you yourself are not laughing, how are you going to know what ripples of health, well-being are created by it? But they must be afraid: if you cooperate and you feel good, you cry and you feel good, and after a whole group you come out more radiant, it is going to destroy your profession. Then rather than giving medicines to people, you can send them here to be healed without any medicines.

Medicines have after-effects: they may heal one thing and they may create another process of sickness. Laughter cannot do that, and the only research done has not been done by Sushrut, has not been done by ayurvedic physicians; it has been done in the Soviet Union and in America and the experimenters agree that people should laugh more, should cry more. This will keep them younger, this will give them longer life.

But these two physicians have not even been around here to see that just the sound of Yaa-Hoo and a tremendous joyfulness, a silence spreads in the hearts of participants. Not of observers – observers are not welcome, observers will be a disturbance. When everybody else is relaxed they will be sitting like a rock amongst the relaxed people. Their very presence will be corruptive.

I will not allow anybody here to be an observer only. Real observation is within yourself: what happens when you let go, when you relax, when you laugh for no reason at all, or you cry and weep just out of a deep unburdening process – which has been triggered by the word *Yaa-Hoo*. And when I have used this word, I have not used this word without going through it and all its implications.

So I won't allow any idiot to criticize it without experiment. He can do the experiment in his own home. All the ayurvedic physicians can get together and cry if they cannot come here – that would be better – and if it destroys the mind, so far so good.

Setcho says, *The empty hall resounds with the voice of the raindrops. Even a master fails to answer.* Not that the master *cannot* answer, but because only silence *is* the answer.

Jesus is standing before the Roman governor of Judea, Pontius Pilate. Pontius Pilate feels sorry for this young man. He is only thirty-three, has not seen much of life, has not committed any crime. Crucifying him seems to be absolutely unjust, but the whole crowd, the mass is asking that this young man should be crucified "because he is corrupting the minds of our people."

This is an ancient blame, placed on anybody who brings any insight into life. Howsoever small an insight – to change, to bring the new in, to open new doors, new mysteries, and immediately the guardians of the old are ready to destroy the person.

Pontius Pilate was a very cultured man, and being a

Roman he was not part of the crowd of the Jews; he was a foreigner, he had no interest in crucifying this young man. He came close to Jesus and asked him, "I know you are innocent and I know the crowd is simply mad, prejudiced; you have in some way offended these people. I have heard many times, particularly my wife has heard you speaking here and there, and she has reported to me. I always wanted to ask, what is this truth that you talk about? Just tell me, what is truth?"

And Jesus looked into the eyes of Pontius Pilate without answering.

You can say without answering, or you can say he was answering with his silent eyes.

Truth is a silent experience.

There is no way to bring it into language.

So when Setcho says, *Even a master fails to answer,* it does not mean that the master is ignorant, it simply means the master knows that any answer will destroy itself, will commit suicide itself. There are questions which are fundamental; they can be answered only by not answering them. *If you say you have turned the current.* If you say you have gone against existence…. *You have no true understanding. Understanding? No understanding? Misty with rain, the northern and southern mountains.* A real master will simply sit silently, listening to the wind coming from the mountains, listening to these bamboos chitchatting amongst themselves.

Setcho is right.

Maneesha has asked: "Osho, I wish I could tell Setcho that in our assembly, 'An empty hall resounding with the voice of raindrops,' is our master's answer."

Maneesha, if you meet Setcho somewhere, some day... and it is almost possible. In eternity we come across the same people again and again; there are not many more people, they just come with changed faces, sometimes growing a beard, sometimes shaved....

If you meet Setcho, certainly say what you are saying: "An empty hall resounding with the voice of raindrops is our master's answer." It is not only your master's answer, it is *the* answer.

Her second question is: "You have never failed to answer – or at least whenever I have listened for it, I have always heard a response. What is your comment?"

Listen to the bamboos....

[*Osho waits for the bamboos, but at this moment they sing very quietly.*]

These bamboos are mischievous fellows! When you are ready to listen to them, they become silent. And when nobody is listening they are telling great truths.

[*The bamboos answer – very loudly!*]

Perfectly good!

Her third question is: "When one's voice becomes the voice of the raindrops is that your constant milieu?"

Maneesha, when one disappears, leaving behind only a pure consciousness, then raindrops or no raindrops, then bamboos or no bamboos, just a pure awareness of whatever goes on around is certainly my milieu – and I want it to be your milieu too.

The very air, your very presence should be a constant silence, because only in this silence blossom all kinds of roses.

Now something particularly for the bamboos; a few of them are bananas...

A man and his dog are watching a movie. The dog barks for the hero, growls at the villain, and howls during the sad parts.

A man in the next seat leans over, "That's amazing!" he says to the dog's owner, "Your dog really seems to be enjoying the movie!"

"It *is* amazing," says the owner, "he *hated* the book!"

Hymie and Becky are celebrating their twentieth wedding anniversary by going to see a movie. It is a hot, steaming, passionate film, and it arouses the animal instincts in Becky. When they get home that night, she snuggles up close to Hymie, but he ignores her.

"Why is it," cries Becky, "that you never make love to me like that hero in the movie?"

"Don't be stupid," snaps Hymie. "Do you know how much they pay those guys for doing it?!"

Mother Superior is talking to three teenage girls who are about to leave her orphanage.

"You are going into a wicked world!" she says. "Men will try to take advantage of you. They will buy you drinks, take you to their apartments, and do terrible things to you. Then they will give you twenty dollars and kick you out!"

"Excuse me, Holy Mother," says one of the teenagers, "but do you mean these men will take advantage of us *and* give us money?"

"Yes, my child," sighs the nun. "Why do you ask?"

"Well," replies the girl, "the priests only give us candy."

Kowalski wants to go moose hunting in the wilds of Canada. So he arrives at a small trading post to buy some equipment.

The storekeeper advises Kowalski to hire Bruno, the greatest moose-caller in the country.

"It is true," says the storekeeper, "that Bruno is expensive, but he has a sexy quality in his voice that a moose finds irresistible!"

"What does he do?" asks Kowalski.

"Well," explains the storekeeper, "Bruno will make his first call when the moose is five hundred meters away. When the moose hears it, he will be filled with desire and approach to two hundred meters.

"Then Bruno will call again, only this time, he will make it more suggestive. The moose will rush closer, and then Bruno will make his sexiest call. The moose will become inflamed with carnal desire and come to a point just a few meters away.

"And that is the time, my friend, when you shoot!"

"Suppose I miss?" says Kowalski.

"Ah," sighs the storekeeper, "that would be a catastrophe!"

"But why?" asks Kowalski.

"Well," replies the storekeeper, "then Bruno gets screwed!"

Now, two minutes of silence.
Close your eyes, be absolutely frozen, contain your energy within yourself...

Now relax.

Okay, come back.

THREE POUNDS OF FLAX

Osho,

Tozan's Three Pounds of Flax
A monk asked Tozan, "What is Buddha?"
Tozan said, "Three pounds of flax."

Setcho says:

The golden crow swoops, the silver hare bounds;
The echo comes back, direct and free.
Who judges Tozan by his word or phrase
Is a blind tortoise, lost in a lonely vale.

The abundant blossoms, the luxuriant flowers,
The southern bamboo, the northern trees.
One recalls Riku Taifu and Chokei:
"You should not cry, but laugh!" Eh!

Osho,
Yaa-hoo!

Maneesha, not finding any expression for truth, Zen has developed a language of its own; hence, to ordinary logic it looks absurd. But those who have experienced their own being, their consciousness, will find that although the language is absurd it is absolutely relevant.

Zen's case is very special, for example *Tozan's "Three Pounds of Flax."*

It is impossible to say what the experience is of being a buddha, of being awakened. Even in your common life you wake up every morning, you go to sleep every night; thousands of nights you must have slept and thousands of mornings you must have awakened – but can you describe what sleep is? You cannot say, you don't know it. Can you give any explanation to the experience of waking up in the morning? You have known it many times; it is not something unknown to you. But still, when it comes to expressing it you come up against a very adamant wall: the language that we use for communication simply fails. But something has to be done. The question has been asked, an answer has to be given and the language does not allow any answer.

In such a situation Zen developed its own language. It can be easily criticized, condemned, described as absurd and irrational, but that is not very intelligent. Intelligence needs to find a way to understand the irrational language of Zen.

A monk asked Tozan...

Tozan is one of the most significant masters who lived fourteen hundred years ago. He is being asked,

"What is Buddha?"

The word *buddha* is from Sanskrit, but now it has been taken over by the Chinese, by the Japanese, for the simple reason that they could not find anything equivalent. The word *buddha* means a consciousness at its peak. What does it mean – a consciousness at its peak?

*Tozan said...*You must be expecting some philosophical answer, some theological answer, some rational explanation, but what Tozan said is,

"Three pounds of flax."

At that moment he was carrying three pounds of flax. In that moment he could not indicate anything else; there was nothing else available other than three pounds of flax. In fact he is saying that the question is wrong and if you ask a wrong question you will get a wrong answer. But he is compassionate and polite. Rather than saying, "You idiot! A question about buddha is not to be asked – it is an experience without any explanation, an experience beyond mind." Being of a very kind nature, rather than saying that you are asking a wrong question, he simply gives an absolutely absurd answer: *"Three pounds of flax."*

In that moment it must have come to the inquirer as a shock and also as an insult – not only to himself but to Gautam Buddha – but he knows that Tozan cannot be insulting or derogatory in any sense toward Gautam Buddha, because for Tozan to insult Gautam Buddha will be to insult himself.

His answer is indicative that it is not possible for language to contain the experience. It is almost like, "Whatever I say will not be much more valuable than three pounds of flax."

Try to see the point.

I will give you an example, perhaps that may help you....

Adolf Hitler convinced one of the most civilized, cultured, courageous nations that the defeat of Germany in the First World War and all the problems of Germany were because of the Jews. At first people laughed: "This is absurd! Jews have nothing to do with it; on the contrary, they had given more money to the fight than anybody else, and to make them responsible...." But when somebody continuously repeats a thing it becomes a truth. Every lie can become almost true; it just needs to be repeated with dogmatic, authoritative force.

That was the whole strategy of Adolf Hitler. He was not a man of great intelligence, but he made the whole nation convinced that he was right: "If Jews are removed all problems will be solved."

One day as he was coming from his morning walk he met the chief rabbi of Berlin – a strange coincidence. Adolf Hitler asked the rabbi, "What do you think…what is the cause of Germany's failure, all its problems?"

The chief rabbi said: "It is very simple: the bicycles. Unless you destroy all the bicycles there is no chance for Germany to attain to its glory."

Adolf Hitler said, "Are you joking? What kind of nonsense are you talking? How can bicycles be responsible for Germany's failure?"

The chief rabbi said, "I was just saying that – how can Jews be responsible? And if Jews can be responsible then what is wrong in bicycles…?"

This answer of Tozan's is absurd, but any answer will be absurd. So you have to understand the milieu of Zen. In fact Tozan has not answered, he has simply said to the man, "Don't ask such stupid questions! But because of my kindness, I cannot call you stupid. And all answers possible will be of the same quality as three pounds of flax, which is at least right now available in my hands. I can show it to you."

By his answer he is making all answers useless.

Commenting, Setcho says:

> The golden crow swoops, the silver hare bounds;
> The echo comes back, direct and free.
> Who judges Tozan by his word or phrase
> Is a blind tortoise, lost in a lonely vale.
>
> The abundant blossoms, the luxuriant flowers,
> The southern bamboo, the northern trees.

One recalls Riku Taifu and Chokei:
"You should not cry, but laugh!" Eh!

Setcho is saying that when *the golden crow swoops,* or *the silver hare bounds; the echo comes back, direct and free.* That is the buddha: the echo. *Who judges Tozan by his word or phrase is a blind tortoise, lost in a lonely vale.*

Don't judge Tozan by his word; look into his eyes, feel the dance of his heart. Look at the grace and the compassion and the love of the man.

In his comment he reminds me of an incident with Riku Taifu, one of the disciples of great master Nansen.

Nansen died…. Riku Taifu stood in front of his master's coffin and gave a loud laugh. A priest reproached him, saying, "Wasn't he your teacher? Why do you laugh when you should lament for him?"

Riku Taifu said, "Say a word, and if it fulfills the Buddha's teaching I will lament."

I will repeat: He is saying, "I am ready to lament. Say a single word that fulfills Buddha's teaching and I am ready to lament."

But the priest could not utter a word. Deploring this, Riku Taifu said, "Alas, our teacher has long gone! Nansen would not have remained silent; he would have said something – perhaps absolutely absurd, but still indicating like an arrow toward a faraway star."

And saying this, Riku Taifu wept aloud. Later, Chokei hearing of this, said, "You should not cry, you should laugh!"

Another Zen master, when he heard this, said, "There is no reason to cry: Nansen has fulfilled his destiny. It is a time to celebrate. He has not gone anywhere, he has simply become free from the form of body and mind; he has become just pure consciousness like the air surrounding you. He was confined into the body, now he is unconfined. This is not the time for crying. You should not cry; you should laugh."

That's why poor Maneesha has to shout, "Yaa-Hoo!" That is perfectly good: three pounds of flax or Yaa-Hoo – both weigh three pounds.

There is a strange story that developed in the name of Zen. A small group of people, beginning with Mahakashyapa, at the time of Gautam Buddha...

Although it is called *Zen* Buddhism, Zen should not be attached with Buddhism – it has nothing to do with any *-ism*. It is a pure experience without any theology. Its purity is such that no word can catch it, every word is going to pollute it. Mahakashyapa is the founder, not in the sense that Mohammed is the founder of Mohammedanism, or Mahavira is the founder of Jainism, or Karl Marx is the founder of communism. From the very beginning it takes a strange turn that has never happened anywhere else. It is simply unique; there is nothing else with which it can be compared.

One morning discourse Gautam Buddha came with a flower, a rose, in his hand. It was very strange. Even people who had been with him for twenty years had never seen him bringing anything in his hand. What happened...why had he brought this roseflower? But things became more mysterious as time passed.

Buddha sat in his place, and rather than speaking started looking at the roseflower...and continued....

People's waiting became deeper and deeper – and he went on continuously looking at the flower. There was immense silence.... It must have been similar to the silence that is here, but it became heavy. A moment comes – you can only have a certain amount of silence; otherwise it will crush you. It has a weight.

It became too much of a burden. Nobody was saying anything, Buddha was looking at the flower and nobody had the courage or the guts to ask him, "What is the matter? What has happened? Where is the morning discourse?"

Only one man, Mahakashyapa understood. This was the morning discourse: watching silently, saying nothing, just being aware. It may be a roseflower or it may be anything. Watching without being attached – that was the discourse. But seeing that nobody was understanding, Mahakashyapa laughed loudly.

That was even more mysterious because Mahakashyapa was an absolutely silent man. He was never mentioned before in Buddhist scriptures. He has never said a single word to anybody. He was not a talkative person. He used to sit under a certain tree when Buddha was speaking; for so many years he had been sitting under that tree, that the tree had almost become monopolized. Without anybody saying anything, nobody sat there; everybody knew that Mahakashyapa would be coming and that place was reserved.

This was the first time that this silent man laughed – so loudly that he would have defeated Sardar Gurudayal Singh!

[*From the back of the hall, a tremendous belly laugh from Sardar.*]

Only here we have Sardar Gurudayal Singh. Perhaps Gurudayal Singh may have defeated Mahakashyapa, because being a sardar, he cannot accept any defeat – Mahakashyapa or no Mahakashyapa – but unfortunately he was not present in that assembly. He is *our* joy.

But this laughter of Mahakashyapa is the beginning of Zen – because nobody else understood. Buddha said nothing and simply gestured toward Mahakashyapa to come close for the first time in twenty years! – and gave the roseflower to him. This giving of the roseflower to Mahakashyapa is the beginning of Zen.

Now, language is no longer relevant; now, communication has to find some other way. Buddha's giving the rose to Maha-kashyapa is called the *Seal of Zen*. Buddha confirmed Mahakashyapa's understanding that in that vast assembly of monks only Mahakashyapa had understood the silent watchfulness of Gautam Buddha, that only he could hear the unsaid, that only he could *feel* when others had simply wondered what was the matter.

And even now it is being asked in Zen monasteries, "Why did Gautam Buddha give the roseflower to Mahakashyapa?"

It is just an indication, that "you have understood."

Here begins a new language – mysterious, irrational, absurd, but tremendously meaningful.

There is a great need to see Zen not as a religion, but as a language, a method of communion which is totally different from any other communication method.

Zen began in laughter. It will be good to have a few laughters…

Paddy and Sean are sitting in the pub having a discussion about their wives.

"What do you mean," asks Sean, "when you say you have to think twice before you leave your wife alone at night?"

"First," replies Paddy, "I have to think up a reason for going out. And second, I have to think up a reason why she can't go with me!"

Mrs. Zambini goes to visit a medium. "Can you talk with the dead?" she asks.

"I can do everything!" replies the medium, "card reading, fortune telling, astrology, crystal ball, seances, pendulum …what do you want?"

"I want to speak with my grandmother who died in Budapest," explains Mrs. Zambini.

The medium sits her down and turns out the lights. There is silence and then the sound of the wind and the medium goes into a trance. Suddenly there is a voice: "This is your grandmother, darling!"

"Oh, Granny," cries Mrs. Zambini, "How is everything with you?"

"It is beautiful here," replies Granny.

"How is Granddad?" asks Mrs. Zambini.

"He is very happy," replies Granny.

There is the noise of wind and then Granny speaks again, "I must go now, darling."

"Oh, Granny," cries Mrs. Zambini, "I just have one more question."

"Yes, darling, ask it," replies Granny.

"Tell me," asks Mrs. Zambini, "where the hell did you learn English?"

Father Murphy, Reverend Philpot and Rabbi Nussbaum are playing cards together and gambling in the back room of the pub. All of a sudden a policeman comes in and they are arrested.

In court the magistrate asks Father Murphy, "You are accused of gambling. What do you have to say?"

The old priest looks up to heaven, winks and prays silently, "Oh, God! Just one little white lie! I'll never do it again. Okay?" He then announces to the magistrate, "Not guilty."

"Okay," says the magistrate, "you can go. And what about you, Reverend? What do you have to say?"

The clergyman looks piously to heaven and then bows his head in prayer, "Oh, God! Just one little white lie! I will never do it again," and then says out loud, "Not guilty."

"Very well," says the magistrate, "you can go. Rabbi Nussbaum is next. You are accused of gambling," says the magistrate. "What do you have to say?"

"Gambling?" asks the rabbi. "With whom?"

Newly-wed Barbara wants to make sure that she is doing everything properly. She goes to church and into the confession box, where Father Sullivan is sitting.

"Father," asks Barbara, "is it all right to have intercourse just before communion?"

"Of course, my child," replies the priest, "as long as we don't make too much noise."

Now, two minutes of silence…no movement.
Let the body be absolutely still, like a statue, frozen…

Now, relax…

Now, come back.

NOTHING IS BETTER THAN ANYTHING   **10**

Osho,

Ummon's Everybody Has His Own Light
Ummon spoke to his assembly and said, "Everybody has his own light. If he tries to see it, everything is darkness. What is everybody's light?"
Later, in place of the disciples, he said, "The halls and the gate."
And again he said, "Blessing things cannot be better than nothing."

Setcho says:

It illuminates itself, absolutely bright.
He gives a clue to the secret.
Flowers have fallen, trees give no shade;
Who does not see, if he looks?
Seeing is non-seeing, non-seeing is seeing.
Facing backward on the ox,
He rides into the Buddha Hall.

Osho,
Does everyone have their own separate light?
I can see that in the physical world it is light that
shows us the distinction between two people, and
that in darkness, definitions and distinctions are
seemingly obliterated.
But it seems to me it must be just the opposite in
the metaphysical world – that in darkness or ignorance we have the illusion of separateness, while
enlightenment brings the awareness that one is not
separate from everyone and everything around one.
What is your comment?

The second question:

Feeling myself full of light sometimes, trembling
with energy at other times, the mind is happy to
grasp hold of these experiences as "something" –

after all, it is said, "Something is better than
nothing."
Yet when those moments of nothing are there –
when there is no cognition of who I am or who you
are, when there are no exotic happenings – that is
what the mind can make no sense of: I only know
that that space is, and that nothing is better than
something.

And the third question:

I seem to imagine that if I am not thinking
something, doing something, involved in some
project or other, I am as good as dead; to
participate in life seems to me to be life itself.
But as long as I am doing, I recreate myself
continuously, don't I? – when the whole point is
to die to oneself.
What is your comment?

Ummon's comment about everybody's inner light
is absolutely true. Everybody has his own light. But it is
true only as far as we are talking about it, as far as it is only a
concept. Once it becomes your experience, everything dis-
solves, including you. Then there *is* light, oceanic light, in
which everyone has dissolved like dewdrops.

Ummon's statement, *"Everybody has his own light,"* can be
misunderstood. It is very easy to misunderstand such words
as "his own light." I would not have used that; I would say,
everybody is part of one light. And the part is not separate
nor is it separable, and the part is not smaller than the whole.

The part is equal to the whole.

The dewdrop itself is the ocean.

> Ummon spoke to his assembly and said,
> "Everybody has his own light. If he tries to see it,
> everything is darkness. What is everybody's light?"

Here he is making a significant point: one has to relax to such totality that one is not. Even to be is a tension. When you simply disappear, there is light – your disappearance is the appearance of light. But if you try to see where the light is, in your very effort you miss it. The very effort to try brings your ego, individuality, *you* – and you are darkness. As an ego you will not find any light.

That's what he is saying: *"Everybody has his own light,* but *if he tries...."* The whole question is whether you relax or you make effort, whether you are spontaneously losing yourself in the ocean or trying, because the very trying keeps you separate. *"If he tries to see it, everything is darkness. What is everybody's light?"*

Ummon is talking to his disciples. Apparently, what he says seems to be very contradictory. On the one hand he says, "You are the light" – by making the statement that *"Everyone has his own light..."* his *own.* And then he says, "If you try to see it all is darkness." Have you understood what everybody's light is?

Everybody's light is when everybody becomes nobody.

When you simply disappear and nothing prevails all is light.

Of course it is your own, but *you* are not there.

Of course it is your own, because you consist, you are made of light and nothing else.

And it is not only true about human beings, it is true

about material things too.

The mystics were the first.... For almost three thousand years before science recognized that matter is not matter but light, energy, electricity – different names of light – mystics have been saying that "when we go in there is tremendous light." Kabir says, "When I go in I am surrounded by one thousand suns. The light is so much, unbearable. But it is not hot, it is cool; it is not burning, but giving you more nourishment and more life."

Perhaps nobody in the assembly of Ummon was able to answer him, was able to make some sense out of his contradictory statement. I hope it is not contradictory to you.

You are light when you are not.

You are darkness when you are.

The whole question is of the ego.

But Ummon's disciples perhaps miss the point; hence:

Later, in place of the disciples, he said...

Because nobody stood and said anything, the master himself had to reply.

"The halls and the gate."

These are ways only Zen has used to express things which are intrinsically inexpressible. When he says, *The hall and the gate,* he is saying, the coming and the going. If you go all is light, if you come all is darkness. But Zen has its own way of saying things.

And again he said, "Blessing things cannot be better than nothing."

He is saying, "There is nothing better than nothing – even blessings, blissfulness, ecstasies, cannot be better than nothing." Again he is saying, "If you are nothing, you are light, infinite light. But even a small idea of 'I' is enough to destroy the whole thing."

Setcho comments:

> It illuminates itself, absolutely bright.
> He gives a clue to the secret.
> Flowers have fallen, trees give no shade;
> Who does not see, if he looks?
> Seeing is non-seeing, and non-seeing is seeing.

Here Setcho comes a little closer to Zen. *Seeing is non-seeing* because when you see something, your seeing is filled, just as a mirror is filled by the thing it reflects. Then there is no mirror, but only the reflections. But when there are no reflections, the mirror is. Empty it is – full it is not.

Seeing is non-seeing. What are your eyes, except small mirrors? When you are filled with objects you are blinded by those objects. When you attain to a state when you can see *through*, when your eyes are not only reflective mirrors, when they are transparent, reflections don't deceive; reflections don't become identifications. The eyes – even seeing – remain non-seeing.

Shunyo was asking me one day, "When you speak do you see the people to whom you are speaking?" I don't want to offend you but the truth is, when I am speaking who is there to see? And if I start seeing someone, my speaking becomes polluted. You are here, I feel your presence, I feel your silence, I feel your heartbeat – but my eyes remain absolutely vacant.

Many sannyasins have told me that I look as if I am not looking. It is not "as if," it is exactly so. I am not looking. I am not blind either.

> Facing backward on the ox,
> He rides into the Buddha Hall.

That reference concerns the Ten Bulls of Zen. That is one of the most beautiful stories man has ever created. It is a collection of ten paintings....

In the first painting, the bull is lost, the owner is looking here and there, and there are trees all around, but there is no sign of the bull.

In the second picture, he recognizes deep in the forest just the tail of the bull. It indicates that perhaps the bull is hiding there behind the trees.

In the third picture he sees the footprints of the bull, going toward the same direction where he can see the tail of the bull.

In the fourth he has seen the whole bull.

In the fifth he has caught hold of the bull.

In the sixth he has managed to ride on it.

In the seventh he is coming back toward home, sitting on the bull. In the eighth he has put the bull in the stall from where he has escaped.

In the ninth he is sitting by the side of the bull, playing on the flute. These nine paintings are existent in Zen as it exists in Japan, but the original collection was Chinese....

The last painting is missing in these paintings, and the last painting is the most important. It is not just by accident that this painting is missing. It has been dropped deliberately, considering the implications of it. It is a dangerous painting because in the tenth the man is going toward the market-place with a bottle of alcohol.

What are you going to do after you become enlightened? That's what I was saying to you…after a few minutes one starts feeling thirsty, it is time….

The tenth was of immense importance; it says that even when you have found the bull – which is symbolic of finding yourself – it does not mean that you become superior to other human beings. When you have found yourself, rather than becoming superior to others, for the first time you understand humbleness and you start moving toward the marketplace: to the lowliest, humblest, toward the pub where people are drunk. Your buddhahood does not make the drunkards condemned, but you yourself start moving toward the pub to make friends with the condemned, to help them come out of their drunkenness. And that is the only way to help them, to be with them.

One Zen master in Japan was continuously being sent to jail for small things…stealing. And a great master – even the magistrates respected him. They asked him, "Why do you do this? You have thousands of disciples; even the emperor comes to touch your feet – and you have stolen somebody's shoes…!"

He simply smiled. And his whole life it continued – three months in jail, then two or three months outside. Then again he would find a way…and finally everybody became accustomed to the fact that he is incurable.

But there must be some secret….

The day he was dying, one disciple asked, "Don't leave us before telling the secret. Why did you continue your whole life stealing absolutely unnecessary things? We were ready to offer you anything you wanted; you never asked for anything."

The man, before dying opened his eyes and he said, "The reason was that in the prison are the most drunk, asleep people – murderers, rapists, thieves, all kinds of criminals. I had to be with them to awaken them; there was no other way."

This man must have been of immense compassion.

But, afraid it would be misunderstood, when this series of paintings moved from China to Japan the tenth picture was dropped. You will also agree that it does not look good that Gautam Buddha is going toward the pub....

A professor used to come to me – he was a professor in the same university as I was, and he said, "I would like to be a sannyasin" – he was immensely impressed – "but the only fear is that after becoming a sannyasin I cannot go to the pub, and you know that I am addicted to alcohol. Wearing the robe of the sannyasin it will look very weird and other drunks will start laughing."

I said, "There is no harm. Drink anyway. Become a sannyasin and give it a try."

He became a sannyasin and the second day he came – "You have put me in trouble. I was thinking there is only one trouble, the pub; there are many. My wife now touches my feet! She says, 'You are so spiritual!' Now I cannot relate with her in any other way, except by giving her a blessing."

He was very angry, he said, "You! You must have known and still you did it to me – and I have been your friend for so long. Last night in the dark I sneaked toward the pub, hoping that everybody must have left by this time, but the bartender was there. He immediately fell on the ground, touched my feet and he said, 'What a great transformation!'

Now I feel like killing you!"

I said, "It is strange...you asked for sannyas. It certainly brings troubles, but if you can be a little patient it will also bring blessings, ecstasies, which are far more important than the wife or the pub or your friends."

He said, "I *have* to be patient because I cannot go backward; that would be very humiliating."

Afraid of this situation, the Japanese masters who had brought the paintings from China dropped the tenth painting. But because it is still called the "ten" paintings of Zen, the "Ten Bulls of Zen," I became curious because when I counted there were only nine. I had to work for years to find out that they are not Japanese, they are Chinese. They still carry the old title but the tenth painting has been dropped.

Just the consideration that if people become enlightened and still go to the pub to drink alcohol, or go to the gambling places...it will be very difficult to protect their respectability. Just to protect their respectability they thought it was better to drop the tenth painting completely: Don't take it to Japan; only nine are perfectly good. You have found yourself – now play on the flute, enjoy....

But just the flute will not do. To enjoy, many more things are needed – and that tenth painting contains many more things.

Now, sitting here is Zareen with little Farrokh. She became a sannyasin.... She knew and I knew that even though she has a beautiful husband, a very understanding man, but still the relationship has changed. She has moved to the ashram – now, between the husband and herself the old bridge is broken. Because he is a nice and understanding man, they will remain friends – but husband and wife they cannot be. And the little Farrokh is sitting by her side – Neelam was not allowing him to come to the discourse for so long, and he is sitting so buddha-like....

[*Osho turns to his very left where Zareen and Farrokh are sitting and smiles at Farrokh who responds by placing his forefinger on his lips.*]

He has been told not to speak, so he is telling me: Don't disturb.

Okay, Farrokh?

The first question: "Does everyone have their own separate light?"

No, Maneesha.

Everyone has light but it is not separate. We are all one continent. Nobody is an island. We are all together in our innermost being.

Maneesha is asking, "I can see that in the physical world it is light that shows us the distinctions between two people, and that in darkness, definitions and distinctions are seemingly obliterated. But it seems to me it must be just the opposite in the metaphysical world – that in the darkness or ignorance we have the illusion of separateness, while enlightenment brings the awareness that one is not separate from everyone and everything around one. What is your comment?"

My comment, Maneesha, is that what you are saying is intellectually right – "theoretically speaking" that nobody is separate. Enlightenment brings one and everything into oneness – but this is all intellectual. Even the idea of inseparability is intellectual. So is the idea of oneness.

Enlightenment simply means you disappear, you become the whole. There is no question of separation or no separation.

There is no question of oneness, because even in the word *oneness* there hides behind it *twoness*.

What do you mean when you say oneness? – you mean twoness. The mystics have avoided using the word *oneness*, but you cannot. In the very nature of intellectual understanding you can go a little roundabout – and that's what people like Shankara have done. They talk about non-duality, no-twoness; they don't talk about oneness. They want to indicate oneness, but they don't want to use the word *oneness* because oneness points toward twoness.

One has no meaning if there is not two, three, four…. If all other digits have disappeared, what is the meaning of one? One has a meaning only in the context of ten digits; otherwise, if there is no nine, no eight…there cannot be *one*. What will it mean? What can you conceive by oneness, if there are no other numbers left?

It is better to agree with Ummon: nothing is better than all the blessings. Rather than saying oneness, it is better to say nothingness, filled with light.

Your second question is: "Feeling myself full of light sometimes, trembling with energy at other times, the mind is happy to grasp hold of these experiences as 'something' – after all it is said, 'something is better than nothing.'"

That is said by idiots! Those who know, will say: "nothing is better than anything."

It reminds me…

As I was a growing child, everybody told me – all my well-wishers, my parents, my uncles, my aunts, my teachers, my professors – "Listen, the way you are behaving, you will end into nothing."

I used to say to them, "That is my very goal."

One of my professors was so much concerned that he would beat his head; he would say, "You don't understand what…. What do you mean by *nothing*? One has to be *something*."

I said, "I don't see any possibility of myself being something. Something is very small and limited; nothing is vast and unlimited. Something is born and dies – is there today and is not tomorrow. Nothing is always, nothing is eternal."

Except nothing, nothing else is eternal.

Maneesha, you must have heard a saying thousands of years old: Something is better than nothing. But I say to you:

Nothing is better than anything. *Not to be* is the greatest experience.

You are asking, "Yet when those moments of nothing are there – when there is no cognition of who I am or who you are, when there are no exotic happenings – that is what the mind can make no sense of: I only know that that space *is*, and that nothing is better than something."

Make it a point of remembrance that when the mind can make no sense of anything, you are very close to truth. When mind can make sense of something, you are very far from truth. The mind can make sense only of things which come within its boundary – and it has a very limited boundary. Truth is not within its boundary, it is beyond it. It is transcendental, it cannot make any sense of it. So rejoice! When your mind cannot make any sense of something, just rejoice; you are coming closer to home.

And your last statement is absolutely true: "I only know that that space *is*, and that nothing is better than something."

Now you have come to your senses. Nothing is not only

better, it is also greater; it is not only greater, it is the only thing that is existential.

Pure isness
not limited by any word –
and the mystic rose opens.

The third question: "I seem to imagine that if I am not thinking something, doing something, involved in some project or other, I am as good as dead."

That's perfectly right.

Every day I send Shunyo to find out whether Anando is still alive or dead. Fortunately, up to now she has never been dead. One day she will be.

When you are not doing something, you don't feel yourself. Your feeling is a reflective feeling; it is as if when you don't look in the mirror, you start thinking, "Whatever happened to my face?" That's why women carry small mirrors in their bags. In the buses and the trains, once in a while they will take the mirror out and look at the face, to see whether it is there or not – because what other proof have you got?

And besides a mirror, all our actions, all our doings make us feel that we are. And the more we do, the more we are.

You are asking, "But as long as I am doing, I recreate myself continuously, don't I? – when the whole point is to die to oneself. What is your comment?"

Maneesha, to recreate oneself every moment is not contradictory to what I say to you: Die every moment. Unless you die every moment, you cannot recreate yourself. There is no other way. The old dies and the new arises. The old leaves fall and the new leaves come. To remain a living, dancing flow of energy, there is only one way, and that is to die every moment, to be reborn again and again, fresh, new, innocent.

What is happening to you is perfectly right, you have just missed the existential situation of re-creation. The very word *recreate* means first you have to uncreate. In order to wake up the very first thing is to be asleep.

In a small school – just a small school like Farrokh is going to tomorrow, for small boys – the teacher is trying to tell them, "Never commit sin, otherwise you will never reach the kingdom of God without his forgiveness."

After one hour's harassment of those small children, she finally asked one boy, "Tell me, what has to be done to reach heaven?"

He said, "To commit sin!"

The teacher could not understand, nor at the first sight will you understand that the boy is right. Unless you sin you cannot be forgiven – and only those who are forgiven enter into the kingdom of God. The boy's innocent answer is absolutely true. If you are good you are worthless as far as God is concerned. What will he do with you? He cannot even forgive you, you have not committed anything. Just go back home, do something stupid and then come back.

So remember it. If you are going to God, make every arrangement so that he can forgive you. Do some stupid things. That is the absolute requirement to be forgiven. God loves to forgive people. The implication is clear: God loves people to commit sin. Unless they commit sin, they cannot become saints. First commit sin, go to the church, pray; slowly, slowly you will become a saint and then torture yourself. Then God, out of compassion that the poor boy is doing too much, will allow you into heaven.

Such a roundabout way. And in heaven what are you going to do? You will repeat the same thing. That is all that you know. Hence, every religion has made arrangements.

In the Mohammedan conception of heaven, there are rivers of alcohol. Water is impossible to find – just like Pune, pure water is impossible. Pure alcohol is available in Pune too...! In heaven there are pure alcohol rivers; bottles won't do! They won't justify the greatness of heaven.

And beautiful girls who never grow in age...Mohammedanism is fourteen hundred years old. Those girls are still sixteen. They were sixteen years old at the time of Mohammed – now they have got stuck, they cannot become seventeen or eighteen. They must feel very weird – fourteen centuries and they have not passed even one year.

Here too, on the earth women pass time in a different way from men. It is said that one should never ask a woman her age; that is the most irritating thing – and a woman never tells the truth, particularly between the ages of thirty-four and thirty-eight. In those four years, no woman speaks the truth. After thirty-four, suddenly one day they become thirty-eight. This is what in physics is called the quantum leap, or in a more non-scientific way, kangaroo leap! They jump from one station to another station. They have never been in the passage between.

In heaven – whether the heaven is Christian or Hindu or Mohammedan or Jaina, it does not matter – they all disagree on everything but about the age of their girls in heaven they all agree. It seems the same girls have been serving old, dead, dirty saints for thousands of years. I simply feel in so much sympathy that I want to dissolve this heaven completely, because it is doing absolute injustice to womankind.

Are those girls made of plastic? I think they are, because in ancient scriptures it is said they don't perspire. Here also women take much care not to perspire, and all kinds of deodorants...but still you perspire. Those deodorants won't do.

Perhaps in the whole world, if there is somebody who never perspires, that person is sitting here! I live in air-conditioning continuously, I move in an air-conditioned car. Here, now, on both my sides there are air conditioners. I can claim to be the only man in history who has not perspired. And I don't use any deodorant.

It is possible that heaven is air-conditioned, but it is not very likely, because air-conditioning is a very new phenomenon and heaven is so old, millions of years old. I don't think that you can even rent a bicycle there.

Maneesha, it is perfectly good. Die each moment to the past and be born again. Each breath that goes out should be your death, and each breath that comes in should be your life. If you can live with so much change, like a river flowing, you are always fresh, you are always original; your clarity is absolute, you are transparent.

You have recognized the first part by saying, "I recreate myself continuously." Now you have to understand the second part, that "I die every moment, with every breath exhaled."

One thing is certain, that no dead person can inhale. Have you seen any dead person inhaling? Only a living person can inhale. But if you only inhale and remain there you won't be alive long, maybe a few seconds. Life wants to change continuously; that's why you cannot stop breathing. You cannot take a holiday saying, "I am getting tired. Thirty years of breathing, just one day, one Sunday, let me rest." But with this breathing you cannot take a holiday. If you take a holiday it is finished, your holiday will become eternity, you won't come back.

Learn to die every moment. Accept that this is what is happening, you just don't understand it. That is what is happening in your body. If you can understand it and live it lovingly, it becomes a dance.

In-breathing, out-breathing, your heart dances. It goes on throwing out all that is dead and goes on taking in all that is fresh and new.

Maneesha has asked serious questions, and now I have to think of little Farrokh and tell something so that he can laugh....

At a rape trial the young victim is asked by her attorney what her attacker had said before he assaulted her.

The girl is too embarrassed to answer out loud, and so she is allowed to write it down.

After reading the note the judge passes it along to the jury. Mendel Kravitz, who is last in the line, has dozed off, so the woman next to him nudges him and passes the note.

Mendel takes the note and reads, "I am going to screw you like you have never been screwed before." Mendel smiles at the woman and puts the note in his pocket.

"Juror number twelve," orders the judge, "please pass the note to me!"

"I can't, your honor," says Mendel, "it is too personal!"

The bank robbers rush into the bank and order all the customers and clerks to get behind the corner. Then they tell everyone to take off all their clothes and lie face down on the floor. One nervous female clerk pulls off her dress and lies down, face up.

"Turn over, Gloria," whispers her friend, "this is a robbery not the office party!"

Police Constable Perkins is pounding the beat one night

along a dimly-lit street.

He sees three parked cars, and goes over to the first car which is bouncing up and down, and shines his flashlight inside.

"Hello, hello!" he says, rapping on the window with his stick, "What do you think you are doing?"

"Oh!" comes a startled voice. "We are doing the waltz!"

P.C. Perkins goes over to the second car, which is rocking from side to side. He shines his light and taps on the window.

"Hello, hello!" he says, "and what are you doing?"

"Ah, we are doing the samba," comes the reply.

Perkins stops at the third car whose springs are squeaking and windows are all steamed up. He raps on the window and says, "I suppose you are doing the 'bossa nova'?"

"No, officer," comes a girl's voice, "I am doing the boss a favor!"

Dennis Dork goes to Doctor Dingle with a painful case of tennis elbow.

"Okay," says Dingle. "Take this bottle home, fill it with a urine sample and return it to me immediately."

"A urine sample?" cries Dork. "How is that going to help my bad elbow?" "Don't argue," says Dingle, "I am the doctor. Just do it!"

So Dork goes home, determined to make a fool of the doctor.

First, he gets his wife to piss in the bottle, then his daughter. Then he goes to his car and puts a bit of engine oil in the bottle. And finally, he goes into the bathroom and jerks off into it.

He returns the sample to Doctor Dingle and goes back

the next morning for the results.

"Well, Mr. Dork," says Dingle. "Four things to tell you: first, your wife is pregnant; second, your daughter has VD; third, your car is about to blow a piston. And last, your elbow will never get better if you don't stop jerking off!"

Now two minutes of silence.

Close your eyes...no movement, as if you have become a statue.
Gather the whole energy inside.

Now relax...

Now come back.

WHAT'S IN A NAME?

11

Osho,

Kyozan Asks Sansho's Name
Kyozan asked Sansho, "What is your name?"
Sansho said, "Ejaku!"
Kyozan said, "Ejaku is my name!"
Sansho said, "My name is Enen!"
Kyozan laughed heartily.

Setcho put it like this:

Both grasping, both releasing – what fellows!
Riding the tiger – marvelous skill!
The laughter ends, traceless they go.
Infinite pathos, to think of them!

Osho,
What's in a name?

And the second question:

It was such a relief when you had Niskriya hit me
the other night both for being "right" as well as
being "wrong."
The relief at finding that right and wrong have no
place here lasted until last night when I managed to
label my being intellectual "wrong," and the whole
silly game started up again.
How exquisite it must be to live in a world where
there is no right and no wrong.

Maneesha, name and form are the two most important
things to be understood, because we live in the world
of name and form. Both are illusory, both are invented. Both

are mind-made, man-manufactured. Reality has no name and no form. If this is understood, then this small Zen dialogue will not be difficult to understand.

It is very extraordinary of Kyozan to ask Sansho's name. Both are enlightened, awakened people. It is extraordinary, because to ask the name is to ask about the illusory and the non-essential.

To ask about the name is to ask about the invented, not the existent.

You were born without a name.

Do you have a name?

The name is just given to you – you never had any name. It is just a label, you can change it any moment you want. It has no substantiality in it; hence a great master like Kyozan, asking another master of the same category, Sansho, his name, is a very extraordinary dialogue.

Kyozan asks Sansho, "What is your name?"

Apparently in this dialogue you will not be able to find any great philosophy. Because our whole education is intellectual, is based on name and form, we take it for granted that everybody has a name.

Kyozan's asking the name signifies in the first place, "Are you awakened yet or still asleep in the world of name and form? Have you realized yet that you are nameless, anonymous? Have you found it, that you are no one in particular?" A very simple question, yet it contains immense significance – but only for those who can understand the language of Zen. For others it is very ordinary. Every day you ask people, "What is your name?"

Sansho could have said, "My name is Sansho"; then it

would not have been a great dialogue. But Sansho said, "My name? – my name is Ejaku!"

Rather than denying, saying that "I have no name"... because even to say that "I have no name" is to accept the reality of I, the namelessness of I. But he could not be caught in the net Kyozan has thrown.

This is Zen play. When two masters meet, they ask questions, they answer questions, they provoke each other's lion's roar. Sansho said, "My name is Ejaku."

Ejaku is not his name; Ejaku is Kyozan's name. Before he became enlightened, before he was initiated, his name used to be Ejaku. His master after initiation gave him the name Kyozan. Sansho did a good play; he said, "My name is Ejaku."

A Zen dialogue has to be spontaneous, outrageous, sudden, unexpected. Sansho was saying something which Kyozan would not have expected at all. He must have forgotten his own name long ago. Many years before when he was initiated, that was his name given by his parents. Hearing Sansho say, "My name is Ejaku," Kyozan said, "Ejaku? Ejaku is *my* name!"

> Sansho said, "My name is Enen!"
> Kyozan laughed heartily.

Because Enen was also Kyozan's name. That was his name in his childhood, a nickname. Ejaku was his official name, Enen was the nickname everybody used in the family, with the friends.

Kyozan laughed heartily because he could see the great perception and insight of Sansho. Sansho has not answered the question about himself at all. Rather than being straight and saying, "My name is Sansho"…it would have been wrong.

No name is true. All names are fictitious.

It happened that during a certain year a few years ago, America celebrated Lincoln's birthday on a vast scale. Perhaps a certain time had passed, a hundred years or two hundred years. In this celebration one man was chosen to play the part of Abraham Lincoln. From all over America many people applied who looked a little bit like Lincoln, but one man was simply amazing. Even Lincoln would have been in a difficulty if he had met this fellow. He was more Lincoln than Lincoln himself. He was chosen.

It was a one-year-long celebration and the man had to go with this drama party around the country, in all the great cities, to play the part of Abraham Lincoln. He learned the part so well…he looked absolutely like Lincoln, but that was not enough. Lincoln had a little stutter, once in a while he stuttered. The man learned how to stutter. It is very difficult to learn. It is difficult if you stutter to learn not to stutter, but to learn to stutter when you don't stutter is even more difficult! But he did well.

One of Lincoln's legs was a little longer than the other, so he limped. And this fellow managed through massage and bodywork and traction to lengthen one leg. He finally managed, and he started limping like Lenin….

[*Laughter at the sudden change of name provokes a twinkle of an explanation.*]

I forgot, because Lenin also had one leg long and one leg short. That was the only similarity between these two great….

For one year the man played the part every day and when

the year ended, the celebration came to a finish, he went home limping, stuttering – everybody thought that he was joking – in the dress which Abraham Lincoln used to wear a hundred years before. One hour passed, two hours passed; then the family said, "Now it is enough, get out of this dress and be yourself!"

He said, "I *am* myself, I am Abraham Lincoln."

They said, "Don't carry the joke too far."

He said, "I am not joking. Who told you I am joking?"

The family was at a loss. They tried to convince him.

He said, "You can see my leg, you can see my language, you can see my dress; it is self-evident that I am Abraham Lincoln. Why are you bothering me? You are not losing anything!"

They said, "We are not losing anything, but it looks crazy – you were just an actor, have you forgotten?"

He said, "What? Who told you I was an actor? I have been president of America!"

Then they thought that he had gone cuckoo. They took him to the psychoanalyst. When the psychoanalyst saw Abraham Lincoln entering into his office, he stood up. He was so much Abraham Lincoln that even the psychoanalyst forgot that Lincoln has been shot dead a hundred years before! Then he realized....

The man's family came and said, "He has been acting; now it has got into his mind that he *is* Abraham Lincoln, and we have been trying in every possible way but he budges not a single inch. So we have brought him to you."

The psychoanalyst tried, but it was very difficult. What can you do? The man says, "This is strange. I am Abraham Lincoln; why are you all after me? Everybody has a name, I have a name, my name is Abraham Lincoln. What is wrong in it? I limp, I stutter, I use the language that was used a hundred years ago...you can measure my height. For one year continuously I have been moving around the country. Nobody has objected."

Just a few years before, scientists had come up with a lie-detector mechanism, to be used in the courts. It is a small mechanism; it is hidden under the chair. The criminal sits on the chair, the magistrate asks him questions and the lie detector which is hidden in the chair goes on making a graph, just like a cardiogram. As long as the person is speaking truthfully, the cardiogram makes a very simple, even and harmonious graph. The moment he lies, the graph goes off the track.

The psychoanalyst thought that it would be good to try that graph on this fellow; he had the machine in his office. First, things are asked about which you cannot lie, so that the graph can become adjusted. For example, "What time is it on the clock on the wall?" Naturally, how can you lie? Everybody can see what time it is.

The psychoanalyst asked, "How many fingers do you see on my hand?" Naturally you cannot lie. Simple questions in which it is impossible to lie, so the graph can become harmonious, and then suddenly he asked, "What do you think, is it true that you are Abraham Lincoln?"

And he said, "Of course." And the graph went on without any change. Even the psychoanalyst could not believe his eyes that this man has not only become mentally identified with Abraham Lincoln, it has even reached to his heartbeats. He was dragged from this analyst to that analyst. Finally he became tired. He said, "This is stupid, why should I be unnecessarily harassed?"

But the whole village became interested. Everybody was

saying to him, "You are not Abraham Lincoln. Forget all about it. That was just acting."

Somebody reported to the court that this man was deceiving. He was brought into the court. Seeing the situation…he was getting tired. He was put on that lie-detector mechanism again, and when it was asked, "Who are you?" he said, "I am not Abraham Lincoln, I am tired of it." But the graph said, "No, he *is*." The graph did not accept his denial of being Abraham Lincoln because he was only denying intellectually. Deep down he knew who he was. The graph picks up the very heartbeat, your innermost feeling, not what you say but what you feel.

We have all become names, but we were born nameless and we will die nameless. But such is the deceptive way of the world that you will live with a name and even when you die, people will put the name on your grave. There was no such name ever as a reality; it was a fiction. A nameless reality existed, a nameless reality changed its form, but the grave will carry for years, as long as it remains, a name which represents nobody.

Kyozan asking Sansho, *"What is your name?"* is provoking him. If he says, "Sansho," then he has not realized the nameless reality. If he says, "I am not Sansho," then the question arises, "Who are you? – You must be somebody."

Even in denying he is accepting somebodiness; there must be some other name: "Just tell it exactly – what is your name?"

But Sansho was not to be caught by Kyozan's game. He was of the same perceptivity and clarity; he reversed the whole process. He said, "My name? My name is Ejaku."

He diverted the whole thing, he got out of the net completely. Kyozan said, "Ejaku? Ejaku is *my* name!" Sansho said, "Perhaps, then my name is Enen!"

Seeing the situation, that it is difficult to get hold of this man in a wrong statement....

Both the statements were wrong; according to anybody both the statements are wrong. If he had said "Sansho," in your eyes that statement would have been right. But in Zen things are different; it is a totally different atmosphere of seeing things.

Kyozan, feeling that he cannot be caught – he is throwing the net back on him – laughed heartily. This laughter accepted that Sansho is as enlightened as Kyozan. Nothing was said, but that laughter is the seal of recognition.

Setcho remarks:

> Both grasping, both releasing – what fellows!
> Riding the tiger – marvelous skill!
> The laughter ends, traceless they go.
> Infinite pathos, to think of them!

Setcho is making a beautiful statement about the dialogue: What great fellows, provoking each other to fall into a state of ignorance or to make a statement that is not right. And when it could not happen, then there was just laughter. And laughter leaves no trace behind: *The laughter ends, traceless they go.*

Just like laughter we come and just like laughter we go.

Maneesha is asking, "Osho, what is in a name?"

The whole world, the whole world that you know. But it

is all dream stuff. If you remain confined to names, you will never know the reality. Existence is nameless. All names are given by us.

There was one man in India.... There were only two persons who were called Mahatma: one was Mahatma Gandhi, another was Mahatma Bhagwandin. I never agreed with Mahatma Gandhi, but with Mahatma Bhagwandin I had a great friendship. He was very old and I was so young, but we both felt some synchronicity. So whenever Mahatma Bhagwandin used to come to my city, he used to stay in our house. He was a great scholar and immensely informed. I have never come across anybody who is so informed about so much rubbish. You ask him anything and he will function almost like the *Encyclopedia Britannica.*

I used to go for a morning walk with him, and he would tell me about every tree: its name, its Greek name, its Latin name, its ayurvedic qualities, its medicinal purposes, its age.... The first time I tolerated it; the next day when he started again I said, "Please! Because of your knowledge you cannot enjoy the walk. These beautiful trees become covered with Latin words, Greek words, Sanskrit roots, and I am not interested to know. It is enough for me that the tree is dancing in the wind, and I can hear the song and the joy. And I certainly can say that you cannot hear, you are deaf. You are a great encyclopedia, but you are not a conscious human being."

He was surprised, shocked. For half an hour he remained silent; and then he started again. As he came across a tree he said, "Look, this is the only tree that exhales oxygen in the night and inhales oxygen in the day."

I said, "My God, I have told you that I am not interested. It is enough for me that the tree is green, full of flowers and looking so beautiful in the morning sun...the dewdrops are still on the leaves. You destroy the whole beauty, you don't have any aesthetic sense! And you are an old man – you are my grandfather's friend, you are not my friend; the distance of age between me and you is half a century as far as years are concerned. But if you think of consciousness, the difference between me and you is many, many centuries!"

He said, "You are strange; I wanted to make you more informed. In life one needs knowledge, information about everything."

I said, "Who is going into that life where knowledge is a commodity, where knowledge is sold, purchased? Who is going? My interest is not in the world of names. My interest is in the hidden splendor which you are completely forgetting because of your knowledge. You are covered with your knowledge – so thick that you cannot see the light, the joy of anything. Your knowledge becomes a China Wall."

I thought he must be angry, but on the contrary – he was a very sincere man – he reported to my grandfather, "Although he has insulted me again and again on my morning walk I am not angry. I am simply happy that his interest is not in the names but in the nameless. In seventy years nobody has told me" – and he was respected all over India as a great saint – "nobody has told me, 'You are wasting your life in accumulating knowledge.' This child has made me aware that I have wasted seventy years. If I live a little longer I will start learning again so that I can have some acquaintance with the nameless, with the formless, with that which is."

It happened by chance, that the day he died I was present. He died in Nagpur; I was passing from Chanda to Jabalpur. Nagpur was just in the middle, so I asked the driver to take me to Mahatma Bhagwandin, "just for half an hour and you can take a rest."

I could not believe it when I saw him. He had become an absolute skeleton. I had not seen him for almost five years.

He was dying but his eyes were showing a tremendous light. He had become only eyes; everything else had become dead, just a skeleton.

Looking at me he said, "It cannot be coincidence that you have come at the right time. I was waiting, because I wanted to thank you before I leave the body. These years have been difficult in dropping knowledge, information, and finding that which is hidden behind names. But you have put me on the right track, and now I can say all names are false, and all knowledge may be useful but is not existential, is not true. I am dying with absolute peace, the silence which you have been talking about again and again."

I had to delay because it seemed that he was going to die within a few minutes, or maybe a few hours at the most. Within five or six hours he died, but he died with such peace, with such joy. His face was so blissful, although his whole body was suffering from many diseases. But he had already got disentangled from the body; he had found himself.

You are asking me, Maneesha, "What is in a name?"

Nothing, it is just a utilitarian labeling; otherwise, it would be difficult to find where Maneesha is. If I ask somebody, "Where is...that isness, that reality?" It will be difficult. It is absolutely useful to have a name. The problem arises when you become the name and forget yourself. If you remember that you are not the name, if you remember that you are not the form, the body, if you remember only that you are a pure consciousness, then there is no harm. Use the body, it is a beautiful mechanism; use the name, it has its own purpose; otherwise the post offices will be in difficulty, all the letters are coming to nameless persons. You will be in difficulty finding your own home, finding your own wife in a crowd, where everybody is, but nobody has any name. You may shout, "Hey!" but that is applicable to everybody.

Remember: what is utilitarian is not necessarily existential and what is existential is not necessarily utilitarian.

One of my professors used to tell me again and again, "What will you do by finding the truth? Find something else – money, power, prestige, respectability. Find something else. What will you do with truth?"

I said, "You are right; truth has no utility. It will not make you more respectable; on the contrary, your truth may take you to the cross. It may make you more condemned. Wherever you are, people will avoid you: 'This man has truth, avoid!'"

Truth is a very contagious disease. People have their lies, comfortable lies, and when they come to encounter a man of truth all their lies start falling down. And those lies are their whole life, their earning, their success, their money, their power.

The man of truth is avoided, and if he is stubborn then he has to suffer the fate of Socrates: the society poisoned him – or he has to suffer the fate of Jesus: the society crucified him. In India we have not crucified Gautam Buddha because we know better. It is an ancient land, the most ancient land in the world. It has learned that crucifying does not help; on the contrary, it is creating a trouble. By crucifying Jesus, Christianity was created. If they had contained them-selves and tolerated – he was not doing anything – if they had allowed him to talk, there would have been no Christianity. But the crucifixion created Christianity; the crucifixion became the sanctification of the truth of Jesus.

India knows better. It crucifies in a very sophisticated way:

it starts worshipping. It says to Gautam Buddha, "You are God, we will worship you. We will not follow you because we are ordinary human beings. You come as an incarnation of God. We are not of the same category so it is good for you to say great things. We will hear and we will bring coconuts to offer you. We will make your statue, we will raise temples for you."

Nobody thinks that this is another kind of crucifixion: a very sophisticated crucifixion, far more successful, because Hindus accepted Gautam Buddha as a reincarnation of God, but Buddhism disappeared from India. The same brahmins, the same Hindus against whom Gautam Buddha was fighting ...fighting against their Vedas, their Upanishads, fighting against their whole ritual...rather than becoming enemies of Buddha, the same brahmins – their sophistication is worth understanding – declared: "He is an incarnation of God. What he is saying, don't contradict. Worship him, but don't follow him because whoever is going to follow him will fall into hell."

Hindu scriptures say that Gautam Buddha is an incarnation of God. He is here just to test your trust in Hinduism. Such cunningness, such sophisticated....

In *Shivapurana*, one of the Hindu scriptures, the story is that God created the world, created heaven, created hell, made the devil to take care of hell. But millions of years passed and nobody came to hell. Because people were virtuous, they were all going to heaven. The trains going toward hell were all going empty. Finally, the devil became very irritated and he went to God and said, "You can appoint anybody else as governor-general, I am perfectly disappointed in you. For what have you made me take care of hell? Nobody comes there. I am sitting alone, not even a single soul to chitchat with!"

God said, "Don't be worried. You go back and I am coming into the world as Gautam Buddha to corrupt people's minds, so that they can start falling into hell."

As Buddha died Buddhism disappeared, because who is going to fall into hell? They will worship Gautam Buddha but they will not follow him. They will make his temples and his statues – and there are more statues of him than of any other man in the whole world.

In Arabic even the name of Buddha has become synonymous with statue, *budh*. *Budh* is a deformation of *Buddha*; *budh* means statue. There are so many statues of Gautam Buddha all over the world.... In China there are temples with thousands of statues of Buddha. One temple has ten thousand statues – the whole mountain has been cut into statues.

Hindus proved really cunning. The Jews were simple in the sense that they crucified Jesus and unnecessarily created a calamity for the whole of humanity. Now half of the world is Christian and the Jews are responsible for it because they crucified an innocent young man, just out of his mind, talking great things, knowing nothing. Nobody in the world has said...in all these four million years humanity has been in existence, nobody has dared to declare, "I am a son of God," or even a faraway cousin. Nobody has even seen God himself. People are searching for God, and Jesus is declaring, "I am the only begotten son. Forget about God, I will take you into the kingdom of God, my father's kingdom."

Even though these were stupid and nonsense statements, they don't deserve crucifixion. You could have laughed, you could have enjoyed, you could have entertained yourself: "Look at this fellow, he is the only begotten son of God. Sitting on his donkey, followed by a few fools...." But there was no need to crucify. I cannot conceive that to crucify this fellow can be justified in any way. He may be wrong, but that does not mean that if somebody is wrong it makes two plus two equal to five. It does not mean that you have to crucify him.

You have to correct him. If somebody says, "I am the only begotten son of God," you have to take care of him, take him to a psychiatrist, to a hospital, bring him to his senses. Crucifixion is not the right thing to do with such a fellow, because that crucifixion will create ripples which you will not be able to control.

India has seen many, many people of far greater and stranger philosophies, declaring themselves as incarnations of God. But India has said, "Perhaps – no harm, enjoy the idea!" But nobody has been crucified.

Just those who believe only in language and don't see the reality behind it, they make the name too important; otherwise a name has no importance.

Second question: Maneesha says, "Osho, it was such a relief when you had Niskriya hit me the other night both for being 'right' as well as being 'wrong.'"

First I have to correct you. I had told you – but I am a man who forgets things, my memory is not good – so I had told you that Niskriya will hit you. Whether you are right or wrong does not matter because in the world of pure existence nothing is right and nothing is wrong, everything simply is. So I had said it, but I forgot actually to order Master Niskriya to hit you. So what has not happened yesterday, will happen today. What does it matter?

Master Niskriya!

[*Niskriya wants to take his feather, but...*]

No! Not your peacock feather, Maneesha needs a real hit. Stand up! And where is your staff?

[*Niskriya, embarrassed, shows his empty hands.*]

Now find out some way to hit her.

[*He takes Maneesha's microphone and taps her head with it.*]

Right.

It is true, Maneesha, right and wrong are our ways of religion, morality, they are our own inventions; otherwise, existence knows no distinction between right and wrong. Right and wrong are our mind distinctions. And because of these distinctions humanity cannot become one and has to suffer wars, has to suffer unnecessary misery.

For example, someone who has been born into the religion of Jainas cannot accept Ramakrishna as a right man, because he goes on eating fish. In Bengal, the only food people use is rice and fish. But to the morality of Jainism to eat fish, a living being, is immoral and wrong. Jainism cannot accept Mohammed or Jesus or Moses or Krishna for the simple reason that they are all non-vegetarians.

The whole world is non-vegetarian and in fact, even Jainas thinking that they are vegetarians is wrong. They are also non-vegetarians, because trees have life. When you cut a tree you kill a living being. Whatever you eat has come from something living, growing. It may be wheat.... There is no distinction in existence between wheat and fish; both are living beings of different forms. In the whole world there is nobody who is really vegetarian. You cannot be, because the vegetable itself has life of its own.

Either you have to be hungry...but then too you are not vegetarian. Jainas are very angry with me, because I said in their conferences, "Even *you* are not vegetarian because everything is living. It may be cauliflower or cabbage, it may be fish...everything has life."

And they said, "If we don't eat and go on a fast...?"

When I said, "On a fast you are eating your own flesh. Where does your weight disappear to every day? On a fast you lose at least two pounds per day in the first seven days, then one pound per day. Where is this flesh disappearing? You are eating it. Your body needs it, otherwise you cannot live. It is your energy. The body needs a certain energy to move, to breathe, to walk, to talk. From where is that energy going to come?"

If you are a car then you can go to a gas station, but you are a man. We have not yet been able to find some petrol-type thing which is lifeless, so that you have a gas station and you just order how much gas, and a hole in your head.... Even if I move my hand, I am using energy. That energy is coming from where? From your food, from air, your breathing.

If a man goes on fasting, the healthiest man will die in ninety days – that is the healthiest man, which is very rare to find. You won't last that long. The healthiest man simply means one who has so much flesh accumulated that in an emergency he can go on using it without eating. That's why women become more fat than men. But not before marriage, after marriage. They have to become a little fatter – they don't have muscles, just pure flesh, very edible – because they are going to be mothers. To be a mother means to feed a child. For nine months in your womb the child is supplied by the mother's flesh. So the mother is supporting herself and the child, and she needs some emergency reservoir. And even when a woman is not becoming a mother, the tendency of her body is to collect more flesh.

Man is more of a skeleton. The woman has less bones and more flesh; the man has more bones, less flesh. That's why women can fast very easily. For man it is more difficult. The woman has enough of a reservoir. She can feed a child for nine months, she can fast without difficulty, but she is also eating her own flesh. There is no way of being non-vegetarian.

But these concepts create difficulty. Jainas think they are the purest people in the world, because they are vegetarians. Brahmins think that the purest food is cow's milk. And milk is a formation of blood.... That's why when you drink milk you immediately start gaining weight. It is really blood, but according to Hindus it is the purest food, and those who kill cows to eat are wrong. But what are you doing? You are keeping the cows alive to eat. The difference is not much. Somebody is killing the cow to eat; somebody is keeping the cow alive to eat.

And in fact, except man no animal in the world drinks milk after a certain age. Milk is for very small children of any species, because the small child cannot chew anything hard. You will not find a bull drinking milk from his mother, but you will find a great saint, seventy years or eighty years old, drinking milk. This is violence, because that milk was for the cow's own calves, not for Hindu saints.

And more difficulty arises if you understand the chemistry. That cow's milk has a different chemistry from the woman's milk. Cow's milk has a different chemistry. Because it is going to be in the body of a bull it is more sexual. And to drink cow's milk and then try to be celibate....

You can see Hindu mahatmas, they look like bulls and pretend to be celibate. None of them is celibate, because celibacy by itself is impossible. It is as impossible as somebody saying, "I never urinate." He may not be urinating in public urinals, in public places; he may have his private ways, but in some way...if he is drinking water, then it has to come out of the body – unless he is Morarji Desai, who recycles it. Morarji Desai has the oldest urine in the world! And just as old wine is precious, he goes on drinking his own urine, the same urine again and again. It becomes more and more intoxicating. It would be better to drink somebody else's urine; at least it will be fresh!

Drinking one's own, continuously…it is so dirty. But you cannot do anything. In this country such people are thought to be great moralists. They need brain operations; something has gone cuckoo. And Morarjibhai is angry with me, because I told him face-to-face, "You are the dirtiest person in the world. Everybody has fresh urine and you have eighty-year-old urine. Recycling…what kind of nonsense is this?"

But Hindus drink cow urine and it is thought to be very religious. Strange! They will not drink the bull's urine. And I have asked them, "When you call the cow your mother, then why don't you call the bull your father?" They were angry with me, and I was simply saying a simple thing, that if you make such a relationship that the cow is your mother, then the bull is certainly your father whether you accept it or not.

It is true that the bull is not a very moral father, a very immoral fellow, but whatever is the case, once you accept the cow as your mother, you have accepted the bull as your father. And do you think this makes you religious, spiritual, or animal? All these distinctions in every country, in every religion, in every race are just man's projections, his own mind.

Just as your mind becomes silent, there is nothing right, nothing wrong. Everything simply is. Those distinctions of morality simply disappear.

Maneesha, as you say, "The relief at finding that right and wrong have no place here lasted until last night when I managed to label my being intellectual 'wrong,' and the whole

194

silly game started up again. How exquisite it must be to live in a world where there is no right and no wrong."

Don't think that there is some other world. You can live in this world. I have lived in this world and I don't have any idea of right and wrong. Yes, I have my likings and my dislikings, but that does not have any moral connotations to it. If I don't eat meat that is my question of liking. If I don't drink wine that is a question of my liking. Those who drink, that is their liking. My liking does not make me superior to them. I am following my liking; they are following their liking. We are both on the same ground.

There is no world somewhere else, where right and wrong does not exist.

It is your mind, *here*!

If you can drop your mind right and wrong disappear.

Then you simply live according to your natural likings, and you don't impose your likings on other people. That is a crime against humanity. Just as you are free to enjoy your liking, everybody else is free to enjoy his liking, and to live his life in his own style.

Maneesha, there is no other world, but there is a possibility of having a different mind, the mind of a meditator. Then *this* very world is the lotus paradise.

Now a few very serious things...

Randy Musthaver picks up Polly, the prostitute, on the street and asks her, "How much?"

"Ten dollars," she replies, "unless you want it Spanish style, but then it is ten dollars extra."

Randy goes for the Spanish style, so they go up to Polly's room and have a great time.

When they are finished, Randy gets dressed and is heading

for the door, when he stops and says, "Well, I really enjoyed that, but tell me, what was Spanish about it?"

"My God," says Polly, "I nearly forgot!"

She then stands up on the bed, raises one arm, snaps her fingers and shouts, "Olé!"

On a full moon evening, Count Dracula walks into a men's store and asks to see some ties.

When the salesgirl looks into his eyes, she becomes hypnotized. Dracula sinks his sharp teeth into her throat and takes a deep drink.

As she wakes up, the girl remembers nothing, and Count Dracula buys a silk tie and leaves the store.

The next night he is back.

"Would you like to try something different tonight?" asks the girl, innocently.

"No," chuckles the vampire, "I want something in exactly the same vein!"

Hymie Goldberg is on a business trip and finds himself having to use a pay toilet in a public building.

He is making himself comfortable, when he notices that the toilet paper has run out.

Seeing a pair of shoes in the next booth, he calls out, "Excuse me, friend, but do you have any toilet paper in there?"

"No," comes the reply, "I am afraid there is not any here either."

Hymie pauses for a moment. "Listen," he says, "do you happen to have a newspaper or a magazine with you?"

"Sorry," comes the reply, "I don't."

Hymie pauses again.

"Well," he says, "how about Ronald Reagan's postal stamp?"

Becky Goldberg comes home from shopping and is horrified to find Hymie in bed with a beautiful young girl. She is about to storm out of the house, when Hymie stops her.

"Before you leave," he says, "I want you to hear how all this came about. I saw this young girl, looking tired and worn out, so I brought her home and made her a sandwich.

"She was wearing worn-out sandals, so I gave her a pair of your shoes that you never wear, because they went out of fashion.

"She was cold, so I gave her the sweater I gave you for your birthday, that you never wear because the color does not suit you.

"Her jeans were also worn out, so I gave her a pair of yours, that were perfectly good until you gained a few pounds.

"Then as she was about to leave, she stopped and asked, 'Is there anything else your wife does not use any more?'"

Now two minutes of silence.

Close your eyes.
Be absolutely still, frozen.

Now, relax...

Now, come back.

LET NO DUST SETTLE

12

Osho,

Seppo's Grain Of Rice
Seppo addressed the assembly and said, "All the great world, if I pick it up with my fingertips, is found to be like a grain of rice. I throw it in front of your face, but you do not see it. Beat the drum, telling the monks to come out to work and search for it."

Setcho says:

The ox-head disappearing, the horse-head appears;
No dust on the mirror of the Patriarch Sokei.
You beat the drum and search for it in vain.
For whom do the spring flowers bloom?

Osho,
Why is the nature of the mind such that it
doesn't know its own limitations, that it thinks it is
indispensable?

And the second question:

The words *witnessing* and *awareness* do not seem
to appear in Zen very much. Is it that witnessing is
the ability to watch the mind running along its track
without being identified with it, while Zen jolts the
mind off its track into the gap of no-thought?

And the third question:

I often have had the feeling that if I could really
hear just one word of yours, really see just one
gesture of yours, really fall into one small gap of

your silence, I would have understood you at last.
Is that so?

Maneesha, it is questioned by many, why the words *awareness*, or *watchfulness*, or *witnessing* do not appear in the Zen anecdotes. The question is relevant...it does not appear in the words and the anecdotes are written in words. You will have to find it between the words, in the silences that happen between masters and disciples, or one master and another master.

Awareness is not something Zen talks about because Zen is awareness.

Zen has nothing to do with any "about."

Philosophy can talk about awareness, thinkers can talk about watchfulness, teachers can teach what is witnessing, but Zen is awareness.

You have to get hold of it; it is always there in every anecdote – but not so visible, not so tangible, not available to language. If you are trying to find it you will not find it, because every finding is by the mind.

If you forget all about finding awareness and just be silent, you have found it.

Zen is pure awareness.

But certainly it is not mentioned, because it cannot be mentioned. Zen wants not to talk about it, but to transpire your heart, to aflame you; to bring you to the tune, the harmony, the music...where awareness will not be something of an object – where you will *be* awareness.

In your absolute silence, when the mind is not there, what remains?

The mind is only ripples of the ocean.

When the ripples are gone the ocean which was not visible

because of the ripples...suddenly you realize you are it.
Where are you going to find it?

> *Seppo's Grain of Rice.*
> Seppo addressed the assembly and said, "All the
> great world, if I pick it up with my fingertips, is
> found to be like a grain of rice. I throw it in front
> of your face, but you do not see it.
> Beat the drum, telling the monks to come out to
> work and search for it."

We live in such a limited way, our eyes don't see much and
our ears don't hear much and our hearts don't feel much. We
live at the minimum, just a small candle flame. The universe
is vast – in fact its vastness is almost inconceivable by the
mind, because the mind cannot conceive anything limitless.
There is no beginning and there is no end; there is no
boundary anywhere where the universe ends, where you
come to a board which says, "Here ends the world." It does
not end anywhere.

Hence all our words – even words like *vastness, infinity,
eternity* – are very small efforts. In the words of Seppo, the
whole world that our mind can conceive, compared to
the whole real universe, is just like a grain of rice. So small
that he says: If I throw it in front of your face, you will not
see it. *Beat the drum, telling the monks to come out to work,
and search for it.*

So small...he is saying, "Our conception compared to the
reality is so small that because of its smallness we cannot even
get hold of it."

I have told you one story of Bertrand Russell, the only
story he has ever written. He was not a storywriter. My own

understanding is that this story has come out of one of his dreams. He was a great philosopher.

The story is that the archbishop of England dies and finds himself at the pearly gates of heaven. Naturally he is expecting a great welcome, angels with harps singing Hallelujah. What he finds is just the opposite: a big gate, so big that he cannot find how high it is; he cannot find its height nor can he find its boundaries. He himself looks at himself and a great trembling arises in him – he looks like a small ant standing in front of a vast door which is closed. He knocks on the door and he knows that his knocks will not be heard. For the first time he recognizes that even though he is the archbishop of England, that does not matter. Before the gate of God he is just a small ant.

But he tries hard, he goes on beating on the door. Finally, a window opens and St. Peter looks at him with one thousand eyes. He shrinks. Just the glare of one thousand eyes is enough to make anybody shrink in deep fear. He wants to say something but he cannot find the words. St. Peter says, "Don't be afraid, whoever you are, wherever you are, because I cannot see you. I have been hearing a small knock continuously for many days, so I thought it was better to look. You just stand up, wherever you are hiding."

Even the archbishop of England thinks, "This is God…one thousand eyes!"

He says, "Father…" and St. Peter laughs. He says, "I am not God, I am just St. Peter! I am a doorkeeper, but who are you?"

He answers as loudly as possible, but it appears as a whisper in that vast space, "I am the archbishop of England."

"England?" St. Peter says. "Never heard of it. Talk sensibly. To what solar system do you belong?"

"Solar system?"

We know that we belong to this sun. This is our solar system, all the planets, the moon. So he said, "I belong to the only solar system there is!"

St. Peter laughed. He said, "He does not understand! There are millions and millions of solar systems and trillions of planets. You will have to give me the index number of your solar system."

The archbishop was a very learned man, but he had never heard that there is an index number!

St. Peter said, "I cannot help. Without recognizing you, from where you have come, who you are, and what is your purpose.... The index number is needed because then I can run to the library of God and ask the librarian whether this index number shows there is some planet in this solar system where some kind of life exists."

The words *index number* were enough! The archbishop woke up. He was perspiring. He realized how small we are and how small is our conception.

By the way, before he woke up he had asked St. Peter, "Perhaps Jesus Christ may be of help. You ask Jesus; he knows us, I represent him in England."

St. Peter said, "Jesus? What are you talking about, who is this fellow?"

The archbishop said, "My God! He is the only begotten son of God!"

St. Peter said, "I don't know anything about.... The fact is, I have not seen God up to now. It is so vast here inside the door...outside is nothing; inside the door it is so vast that you cannot find anybody. I don't know who this Jesus is, I don't know who this God is. All that I know is that I am St. Peter the doorkeeper."

Seppo is saying, if you are searching for truth, please stop. Truth is so vast you will be lost. Rather than searching for any truth, just be yourself.

In your very being you will find the seed of the whole universe.

In your own heartbeat you will find the universal heartbeat.

Setcho's commentary:

> The ox-head disappearing, the horse-head
> appears;
> No dust on the mirror of the Patriarch Sokei.
> You beat the drum and search for it in vain.
> For whom do the spring flowers bloom?

Setcho is saying, *The ox-head disappearing, the horse-head appears...* Rather than simply saying that you are a mirror: one thing appears; one thing disappears.

No dust on the mirror of the Patriarch – one who knows himself, no dust gathers on him.

You beat the drum and search for it in vain – you will not find it. *For whom do the spring flowers bloom?*

Once in a while, Setcho's commentaries come very close to truth. He is saying that you are just a mirror: things appear and disappear; you keep your mirror dustless, clean. For those who are mirror-like clean, the spring flowers bloom.

I have told you the incident of one of Gautam Buddha's disciples becoming enlightened. Everybody else became aware that something had happened because on the disciple flowers went on showering like rain.

These flowers are not the flowers that you see with your eyes, these are the flowers that you feel with your heart. And the more the silence grew, the more the flowers showered.

Setcho is right:

For whom do the spring flowers bloom?

They bloom for you, but you are asleep. They bloom for you, but your mirror is so full of dust you cannot reflect them, you cannot appreciate them – you cannot sing a song in their praise.

Setcho has referred to Patriarch Sokei as a mirror. Patriarch Sokei is also known as Eno and Hui-Neng. Hui-Neng is his more well-known and famous name.

When Sokei's master, the fifth patriarch Obai
Gunin was growing old, he wished to nominate
his successor. Obai's head monk, Shinshu
presented a poem demonstrating his degree of
attainment. It ran:

The body is the bodhi tree,
The mind is like a mirror,
Every now and then dust and polish it,
And let no dust settle on it.

In Zen, whenever a master chooses his disciple, this is the way: anybody who can present a small poetry which contains the truth, will be accepted.

This poetry – *The body is the bodhi tree* – because the flower of awakening blossoms in the body, it has its roots in the body…. *The mind is like a mirror, Every now and then dust and polish it, And let no dust settle on it* – apparently seems to be very great and philosophical. It seems to be that

Shinshu should be accepted as the successor. But he was not accepted. This will show you the depth of Zen and its approach toward life and existence:

Sokei said:

> Bodhi by nature is no tree.
> The mirror is inherently formless.
> There is originally nothing.
> On what then can the dust settle?

Shinshu's poem was beautiful, but has not the depth of Sokei's poem: *Bodhi by nature is no tree....* A tree grows. Bodhi is your nature – it is already there, fully grown. Each one of you is a totally fulfilled buddha. Whether you know it or not, that does not make any difference.

And talking about the mirror is not right, because your consciousness is formless; it cannot be a mirror. And because there is originally nothing, on what then can the dust settle?

With this poem Sokei became the sixth patriarch, the sixth great master after Bodhidharma.

Your first question, Maneesha: "Why is the nature of the mind such that it does not know its own limitations, that it thinks it is indispensable?"

It is natural to the mind, just as it is natural to everything. You have never thought why you don't have four hands. You have never thought why God forgot to put two eyes behind, back lights so there is no need of turning. You simply walk backward, forward....

It is said...

When Henry Ford died and encountered God, he was

very angry with God...the story is very beautiful.

God said, "I understand you are a great inventor. I would like to ask you one thing: What do you think about *my* creation?"

Henry Ford said, "Your creation? It is so full of faults. Just look: you have put only two eyes and forgotten about the back lights! You have not given man a reverse gear so he can go backward in time. If you had given him a gear, young men could go into their childhood or into their mother's womb – or a child could go forward. You have not given man freedom to move in time backward or forward. You seem to be against freedom of movement!"

God was shocked and when Henry Ford said this it is rumored that God had tears in his eyes. Ford said, "You have put the pleasure point in man's body between two exhaust pipes! Is it in any way sensible? The pleasure point should have been put anywhere else, but not where you have put it – it is so stupid!"

I don't know whether the story is true or not, but it seems to be true.

It is just the nature of the mind, just as it is the nature of everything. The roseflower never thinks about becoming a lotus; he does not bother that he is so small. The limitation is indispensable, intrinsically. You never ask for a few spare parts so that if one head gets lost, you can put on another head. You never question. Even the question of spare parts does not arise, that this is not a right system; every car comes with spare parts, every small child should come with a bag carrying for himself small spare parts: spare eyes, spare legs.... Fractures happen, eyes lose their eyesight...if you had spare things with you, you could immediately change. We simply accept the situation as it is. This acceptance is natural.

That's why, Maneesha, the mind never thinks that it has any limitations. It thinks it is infinite – what limitations? It can think of as faraway things as possible. And naturally it thinks it is indispensable. Everybody thinks, "Without me, what will happen to the world?" You may not say it to anybody, but deep down you think that without you, the world cannot run. There will be chaos, everything will be topsy-turvy. It is because of your presence that the sun rises every day; otherwise at least on Sunday it would be on holiday.

The poor fellow, when the whole world is on holiday – and it is *his* day, Sunday – still he has to do his daily job: rise again, move the whole circle, set down again…. For four billion years, since the earth has existed – we don't count the time before it…there was time before it, but for at least four billion years the sun has never been late, never been sick, never been on holiday, never gone on a honeymoon. The poor fellow simply goes on doing the routine work.

But at the deepest core of everybody, the feeling is that "Without me, there will be a vacancy which cannot be fulfilled. I am indispensable; nobody can take my place" – and we know already, we have taken somebody's place!

Before you, so many millions of people have come and gone, sometimes the horse and sometimes the ox. Nothing is indispensable, but it is very fulfilling to the ego to feel indispensable.

We make ourselves indispensable in small ways. We get married. Now you can say to the world, "Without me, what will happen to my wife?" And everybody knows nothing will happen, she will be simply happy, but you are carrying a great burden. Without you, what will happen to the children? Nothing. They will become orphans and Mother

Teresa will get the Nobel Prize. You are unnecessarily hindering Mother Teresa.

Because we cannot prove that we are indispensable to the stars and to the moon and to the sun, we create small relationships: father, mother, wife, and husband, and friends. And we make clubs: Lions Club – what will happen to the Lions Club without you? It will be simply a donkey club; you are the only lion! We create the illusion around ourselves that we are indispensable.

One of my professors never in his whole life went on a holiday. I became his student just three months before he was going to retire. He was known all over the university as a man who had a great love for students – he would not go on leave. Even if he was sick, he would come to teach.

I asked him, "What is the matter? Why have you never gone on any holiday?" I did not expect the answer that he gave to me – he was a very sincere man, Dr. Das – he said to me, "Nobody has ever asked this; everybody just appreciated. You are not appreciating; on the contrary, you are asking, questioning. I have to tell you the truth. The truth is that if I had gone on any holiday, nothing would change, everything would run smoothly and my feeling of being indispensable would be destroyed. I wanted to be indispensable: without me the university will be a chaos. And I knew, it would not be a chaos."

I can understand the poor professor's problem, because he was a bachelor – old, no wife, no children, nothing else on which he can proclaim his indispensability.

He managed it by not going on holiday. The whole university, all the professors felt it, that certainly he was a superior man. Even on Sundays his office would be open. Any scholar who wanted to come on Sunday too, Dr. Das was available. The whole university was closed, just his office was not closed; it was never closed.

When he retired I went to see him off at the railway station and I said, "You are going? Are you not worried what will happen to the university?"

He looked at me. He said, "Don't harass me – at least while I am going away. Nothing will happen, everything will be all right. It hurts me so much that I am going and nothing will happen, and you are making me aware of it. Talk about something else."

I could see that this man, who was a very learned man and very simple, sincere would shrink in Calcutta, somewhere alone. And I don't think he lived more than four or five months. After retirement he became so useless. I know perfectly well that if he had still been in the university he would have lived. There was no sign of death; he was perfectly healthy. But I could just imagine him in Calcutta somewhere in a small room – because a retired professor cannot manage a palace in Calcutta – in some bachelor's hostel: an old man, utterly useless, nobody even comes to say to him, "Good morning, Sir."

The very day he left, I told him, "Be careful not to die too quickly."

He said, "What do you mean?"

I said, "I am simply saying a psychological truth, which psychology now accepts, that retired people reduce their life span at least five to ten years. When they are not retired they have some utility, some meaning, they are needed by someone."

It is one of man's greatest needs to be needed. If nobody

needs you immediately the question arises: Why go on living? What is the point? There is nobody who will cry tomorrow, there is nobody who will come to your grave to put a few roses there. You will be forgotten as if you have never been. How many people have been in the world? Who remembers them? The same is going to be the situation with you, with everybody.

We are just signatures on water. Even before we are complete, we start disappearing.

Nobody is indispensable, Maneesha, but the ego will not accept it; it is indigestible. Once you accept it, that you are not indispensable, you will feel a tremendous lightness coming on you, all burden....

I have been in offices where on every table of the clerks, head clerks, superintendents, there are piles of files – and I know why those files go on growing into mountains. The reason is whoever has more files on his table is more indispensable; without him nothing can happen. Files move so slowly that I have to make a maxim. Just as Albert Einstein has discovered that light moves with the greatest speed, I have to make a maxim that files, particularly in India, move with the slowest speed. Dust goes on gathering on them, nobody does anything, nobody wants to do, because if there is no file on your table, what are you doing here? Who are you? – you lose your definition.

It is good to understand that we are not indispensable, and that our minds are very limited. It will bring you closer to truth.

Your second question, Maneesha, I have already answered. You have asked: "The words *witnessing* and *awareness* do not seem to appear in Zen very much. Is it that witnessing is the ability to watch the mind running along its track without being identified with it, while Zen jolts the mind off its track into the gap of no-thought?"

Maneesha, Zen simply does not give any substantial support to mind.

For Zen, mind is not.

It is not that the mind has to be dropped.

It is not that the mind has to be stopped from functioning. Yes, these things have to be said because you don't know anything about no-mind. Once you have a glimpse of no-mind you will start smiling…"I was fighting with a shadow – the mind was not there."

Your third question: "I often have had the feeling that if I could really hear just one word of yours, really see just one gesture of yours, really fall into one small gap of your silence, I would have understood you at last. Is that so?"

Zen Master Niskriya…

[*This time Niskriya has his staff with him!*]

Yes, a good hit on Maneesha.

[*Niskriya taps her on the head.*]

Right! This is the seal of being right.

Now we can have a few really good things. This Maneesha goes on asking serious questions!

Barbara Beanbag has been to market and is walking home carrying a duck.

A drunk comes staggering along in the other direction, stops and says, "Hey! What are you doing with that pig?"

Barbara looks at him coldly and replies, "This is not a pig, it is a duck!"

"I know," says the drunk, "I was talking to the duck!"

Abraham Grossman, the rich young bachelor, is entertaining a gorgeous woman, Gloria, with dinner in his penthouse.

As his Chinese servant pours the coffee, Gloria asks, "Wu, how do you make such delicious coffee?"

"Me take plenty boiled water," explains Wu, "and stir in coffee, velly, velly slow."

"Yes," says Gloria, "but it is so clear. How do you strain it so cleverly?"

"Me take master's silk socks…" begins Wu.

"What!" shouts Grossman. "You take my best silk socks to strain the coffee?"

"Oh, no, master," replies Wu. "Me never take master's *clean* socks."

Kowalski hears a noise in the garden and goes out to find his dog playing with the neighbor's pet rabbit.

Kowalski manages to get the rabbit out of the dog's mouth, but finds that it is already dead.

He does not want to upset his neighbor, so he sneaks over the garden fence and puts the rabbit back in its pen, so that the neighbor will think it died peacefully at home.

That evening, Kowalski hears his neighbor freaking out in the garden.

"What is the matter?" asks Kowalski, innocently.

"I have just found my rabbit, dead, in its pen," replies the neighbor.

"Oh dear!" sighs Kowalski, sympathetically.

"That's okay," says the neighbor, "it's just that I had already buried it yesterday!"

Moishe Finkelstein has bags under his eyes and looks very tired, as he goes into the doctor's office.

"Doctor," says Moishe, "I dream every single night. Last night it was *terrible*! I was in an airplane, I had my parachute on and we were five miles above the earth, to make a new parachuting altitude record.

"I opened the door, took one step forward, pulled the rip-cord – what do you think happened?"

"I have no idea," says the doctor.

Moishe gazes into the distance and says, "My pajamas fell down."

Now two minutes for silence.

Be still. Close your eyes.
Collect yourself inward, just as if you are a stone statue.

Okay, relax...

Now, come back.

THE GREAT DEATH   13

Osho,

Joshu and The Great Death
Joshu asked Tosu, "What if a man of the great death comes
back to life again?"
Tosu said, "You should not go by night; wait for the light of
day and come."

Setcho comments:

Open-eyed, he was all the more as if dead;
What use to test the master with something taboo?
Even the Buddha said he had not reached there;
Who knows when to throw ashes in another's eyes?

Osho,
You are one who has come back to life from the
great death. Yet we who have not died are not
nearly so abundantly alive as you. Would you please
talk about this?

And question two:

You are like an exotic flower or rare species of
creature whom I have watched and listened to
and tried to find words to describe for the past
fourteen years.
To hear you talk of the state you are in is to feel
endlessly in awe. One of the most intriguing
things about you is that you are always so
absolutely present and at the same time so totally
absent.
Would you please comment?

And the third:

Osho,
Okay...I'm going to lighten up.
For a master of Yaa-hoo and Yaa-boo
what could possibly be taboo?

The death we know is always somebody else. Once we know our own death, pass through it, a tremendous realization arises that death is the greatest fiction.

This realization is called "the great death." Everybody dies, but the small death; only very blessed ones have died the great death. It simply means they die with total awareness, seeing body and mind separating from their consciousness. But the consciousness, the flame of their being is eternal. It goes on moving into new forms and ultimately it moves into the formless.

This small anecdote is about the great death. Zen is always special in its expression. Joshu calls it the great death because it is not death. The great death in reality is the great life.

Only the small death is death.

The difference is of consciousness and unconsciousness. You die unconsciously – this is the small death; you will have a small rebirth. Neither will you know your death nor will you know your birth. If you die meditatively, alert, aware, it is the great death – and great death is followed by great birth.

Knowingly you die, and because knowingly you die...how can you die? Your knowing, your consciousness continues – knowingly you are born. There is no discontinuity between your death and your birth.

Your realization of this ordinarily would be called "the great life," but there is some reason why Zen has chosen to call it "the great death." The reason is that the great death comes first; behind it is revealed the great life. Unless you open the door of the great death, you won't enter into the space of great life.

> Joshu asked Tosu, "What if a man of the great
> death comes back to life again?"

Now another distinction has to be made which is not clear in the anecdote and is not commented upon by Setcho either. But without bringing in another distinction the experience remains incomplete; it is not entire.

There is death. There is the great death And there is the greatest death. In death you die unconsciously. In the great death you die consciously, but you are born again. In the greatest death you only die; you are not reborn, you simply disappear into the immensity of existence – you disperse yourself in the wholeness of the cosmos.

It is because of this fact Mahavira cannot be born again. There is no way for him to get back into any form; he has become formless. But there are meditators who have not reached the ultimate peak but who have some light, some consciousness, that remains while they are dying. They will be born again; they are not yet ripe enough to disappear into the cosmos. They have not learned the whole secret and mystery of life; they have to go on the pilgrimage a little more.

Joshu's question is, *What if a man of the great death comes back to life again?*

His question seems to be relevant, because there is no precedence in which a third kind of death is recognized. He is asking: "I can understand the great death, that you die consciously, but what about a man dying consciously and coming back to life again?"

He is asking about the third distinction, because we have known of many people simply disappearing into air and they never come back again – and there are millions who go on coming back. They never learn their homework; their lives remain mundane and unconscious. But even if sometimes a few people become a little bit conscious, it is better than not being conscious at all. These people will be born – and from their very birth they will show distinctions, uniquenesses, which ordinary children are not supposed to show.

But this is not the ultimate death which everybody is seeking. Only in ultimate death do you relax totally into existence, not to come back. This coming back is not something great; it is coming back to the prison.

Tosu said, "You should not go by night; wait for the light of day and come."

Slowly, slowly you will be getting the taste of the language of Zen. Rather than saying, "You should not die unconsciously," he says, *You should not go by night* – don't go in darkness, don't go blind – *wait for the light of day....* Wait for consciousness, wait for witnessing. Wait for meditation to grow in you and then you can come.

Setcho comments:
Open-eyed, he was all the more as if dead.

That's how a great master is. In his being, death and life have become one.

There is no separation between death and life.

Open-eyed, he was all the more as if dead;
What use to test the master with something taboo?

Such questions should not be asked – that's what Setcho is commenting. Such questions are of such a great depth that there is no way to answer them. Why put somebody in an embarrassing situation? Hence such questions are taboo.

Even the Buddha said he had not reached there – just to avoid the answer. He must have been asked many times in his forty-two-years-long life of teaching. Rather than putting a lock on their mouths, he said to his questioners, "I have not reached there yet, so I cannot answer it." But it is not true, because he has not returned and he cannot return. That does not mean that others cannot become as awakened, as enlightened as Gautam Buddha. It simply means that the unique personality of Gautam Buddha will never be seen again in the world of time and space.

Who knows when to throw ashes in another's eyes?

Setcho is saying, "Buddha is simply throwing ashes into the eyes of the questioner." You cannot deceive an authentic questioner, because the authentic questioner himself knows it a little bit – that death is a fiction, that life is eternal.

But even Buddha is trying to throw ashes into the eyes of the questioner. It must be out of compassion. He does not want you to think much about death; he wants you to think much about life. He wants you to go deeper into life, and death will disappear on its own accord. The more alive you are, the farther away death is. When you are totally alive, there is no death for you. Of course you will not be in a form, you will be a pure isness spread all over the existence. Not confined in a body of any species, just a white cloud floating in the open sky, unconfined to any form.

Have you ever watched a cloud moving in the sky? It has no form, because its form goes on changing. It is free of any bondage to remain in the same form. It is free as far as form is concerned.

It is freedom.

Maneesha's first question is: "Osho, You are one who has come back to life from the great death. Yet we who have not died are not nearly so abundantly alive as you. Would you please talk about this?"

I have been teaching you nothing else except to be more alive, more loving, more singing, more dancing....

My approach is not the approach of Gautam Buddha. His approach is negative. On his path there are no dances, no songs. On his path you will not find any oasis. His path is perfectly right; it reaches, although it is hard.

But when there is a choice, why choose the hard? Why not choose the way of dancing and singing and being aware – and move through gardens where flowers blossom. There is no need to move through deserts where nothing grows.

It was a historical necessity for Gautam Buddha to move through the desert, but it is not for you. What was the historical necessity for him to move through the desert? For twenty-nine years he lived in beautiful gardens, in palaces, surrounded by beautiful women, song, dance...he was tired of it. It all created a kind of negativity because he knew that this is not life. I was not there to teach him that this in itself is not life, but if you just add a little awareness to it, it *is* life – more life. There is no need to go on a desert path.

I am teaching you to reach to the same goal of ultimate death, but I would rather call it ultimate life. That's where my expression and Gautam Buddha's expression differs.

I don't think that his path of negativity has helped humanity very much; in fact, who wants to die? Have you ever asked yourself – do you want to die? An ultimate death, with no possibility of turning back? And for this ultimate death making all kinds of disciplines, rituals, following a thousand and one rules – you will certainly think that this is mad. If in the end you are only going to gain the ultimate death...it doesn't seem right. And that's why Buddhism has not been of as much help as it could have been.

But it was Buddha's individual necessity. He had lived the life of immense luxury – he was tired of it. If this is life then he does not want to live. He moved in the opposite direction to find the truth. But you have not lived the life of Buddha, the luxury that was available to him. You need not be, and you cannot be negative in your approach. Your approach can only be positive.

And if dancing you can reach to the ultimate, laughing, if you can reach to the ultimate, then why unnecessarily go with a British face? There are other faces also! Don't be serious.

But death...the very word makes people serious.

I want you even to dance in your death, to dance and celebrate even in the death of your loved ones. Life and death both should be part of a single festival without any discontinuity.

Your second question is: "You are like an exotic flower or rare species of creature whom I have watched and listened to and tried to find words to describe for the past fourteen years. To hear you talk of the state you are in is to feel endlessly in awe. One of the most intriguing things about you is that you are always so absolutely present and at the same time so totally absent. Would you please comment?"

Maneesha, totality has two sides: the presence and the absence.

You cannot be totally present if you cannot be totally absent at the same time, simultaneously – you cannot choose one. Just the very word *total* includes presence and absence both.

Your understanding is accurate. You have felt rightly that I am present – at the same time I am not present. This has to be your state also. Only then – the meeting, the communion.

Once in a while you have, for a moment, come to the place where you meet me – but soon your mind takes you away. You come very close to the waters and yet you remain thirsty. Your mind takes another route which goes away from the waters.

In this silence you are both: totally present and totally absent.

This presence, this absence, this totality has to become your whole life.

Just because you could get the feel of an ultimate fact, Zen master Niskriya will have to reward you. Such an understanding should not go without reward.

Master Niskriya!

Bring your staff...

[*Master Niskriya gently taps Maneesha's head.*]

Right!

One hit to yourself also...

Good!

Your third question, Maneesha, is very simple. I wonder how you missed the simplicity of it. You say:

"Osho, Okay, I'm going to lighten up... For a master of

Yaa-hoo and Yaa-boo what could possibly be taboo?"

Taboo is the Only Begotten Son of Yaa-Hoo and Yaa-Boo! In this small statement is implied the whole Christian trinity, and in a far better way because the Christian trinity has no woman in it. And without a woman, what have these three guys been doing?

The father is there – but where is the mother? The holy ghost...this holy ghost is a strange fellow! If he can make Virgin Mary pregnant, certainly he is not a woman. So *he* cannot be the mother; in fact, he is Jesus' father. And who Jesus thinks is his father, is his uncle. "Father, uncle and son" – that seems to be more comprehensible, logical.

The trinity that you have made is perfect....

Yaa-Hoo is the father, Yaa-Boo is the mother, Taa-Boo is the son, the *only begotten* son. Here is a whole religion!

Now some irreligious things....

It is a few nights after Christmas. The door of the stable creaks open and three wise men enter.

They are tiptoeing quietly across to the manger when one of them steps into a huge pile of donkey shit.

Looking down at his ruined golden slipper, the wise man clenches his teeth and mutters, "Jesus Christ!"

Mary looks from her baby to her husband, "Hey! Joe!" she says, "that's a *much* better name than Albert!"

Solomon Liebowitz owns a little pharmacy in New York.

One day his assistant, Danny, comes running into the back and cries, "Mister Liebowitz, there is a man in the shop who wants to buy some arsenic to kill himself. What shall I do?"

"Is he a good Jew, like ourselves?" asks Sollie.

"He certainly is," replies Danny.

"Okay," says Solomon "tell him that to kill himself he will need twenty dollars worth. He will soon change his mind!"

One day Lupo is walking home when he notices a huge gorilla standing on the roof of his house.

Not knowing what to do about it he looks in the phone book under *Gorilla Removals*. Then he calls up Kowalski's Get Lost Gorilla Service and explains the situation.

Ten minutes later Kowalski arrives with a banana, a bull-dog, a butterfly net, a ladder and a loaded gun.

"Okay," says Kowalski, "it is quite a simple thing. I am gonna throw the banana at the gorilla, and while he is busy eating it, I am gonna climb up the ladder and push him off the roof.

"Then the bulldog is trained to grab him by the nuts, and when the gorilla holds himself in pain, you throw this butter-fly net over him."

"Great!" shouts Lupo, with enthusiasm.

"But what about the gun?"

"Well," explains Kowalski, "if I miss the gorilla and fall off the roof myself, you shoot the dog!"

The Western Australia Old Ladies' Discussion Group meets each week, but all they ever talk about is cocks and pricks. After a while the ladies get worried because they use the words so much – and they might let them slip out in public. So they decide to substitute the words *prick* and *cock* with other words which won't sound bad if they say them by mistake outside the club.

They write to Old Ladies' Clubs all over the world to ask for advice.

The British Old Ladies' Club writes back and says they

use the word *gentleman* because he always stands up when a lady comes in.

The Italians use the word *curtain* because it goes up when the show begins and comes down when the show is over.

The Americans use *chewing gum* because it goes in hard and comes out soft.

And finally, the French say that they use the word *anecdote* – but with no explanation. So one of the Australian ladies finds a dictionary and looks up the word.

"Here we are," she says to the others: "*Anecdote*: A little story that goes around from mouth to mouth.'"

Now, two minutes of silence.

Relax…

Now come back.

BEAT THE DRUM

14

Osho,

Kasan's Beating the Drum
Kasan said, "Learning by study is called 'hearing'; learning no more is called 'nearness'; transcending these two is 'true passing.'"
A monk asked, "What is 'true passing'?"
Kasan said, "Beating the drum."
The monk asked again, "What is the true teaching of the Buddha?"
Kasan said, "Beating the drum."
The monk asked once more, "I would not ask you about 'This very mind is the Buddha,' but what is 'No mind, no Buddha'?"
Kasan said, "Beating the drum."

The monk still continued to ask: "When an enlightened one comes, how do you treat him?"
Kasan said, "Beating the drum."

Setcho put it like this:

Dragging a stone, carrying earth,
Use the spiritual power of a thousand-ton bow.
Zokotsu Roshi rolled out three wooden balls;
How could they surpass Kasan's "Beating the Drum"?
I will tell you, what is sweet is sweet,
What is bitter, bitter.

Osho,
Would you agree with Kasan that there is a state
beyond learning?

The second question:

Is it possible to hear through the eyes and see with
the ears? That's what feels to be happening during
these discourses.
Would you please comment?

And the third question:

What did the monk mean by his last question?
To speak of how to treat a buddha sounds as if
one has some control over how one will be in his
presence, as if there might be a certain protocol
to be observed.

Would you please explain?

Maneesha, before I talk about the anecdote, I would like... Who is at the drum? Nivedano, beat the drum first.

[*Nivedano hits the drum hard.*]

You will have to do it again and again whenever I say....

This anecdote about Kasan's beating the drum looks so simple from the outside, but from the inside it has tremendous meaning and is multidimensional.

The first....

You have to understand what a drum is.

A drum is emptiness enclosed.

Nivedano...

There is nothing inside the drum. That is our actual state. We are just an outside cover, inside is emptiness. And just as the drum can speak out of emptiness, you are doing everything out of emptiness. This is one dimension of the meaning of Kasan's beating the drum.

The other dimension is that whatever question is asked to him, he goes on saying in answer, "Beating the drum." It does not matter what question you are asking – there may be

millions of questions but there is only one answer:
Nivedano…

…and the answer cannot be verbalized. That's why Kasan
used to keep a drum by his side. You ask him anything – it
does not matter what you are asking, he will simply beat the
drum. That was his answer.

Reduced to your understanding it means, "Be nothing
just like the drum and you will find the answer. I cannot give
it to you, it is your own emptiness. At the most I can hit you
from the outside, but the sound comes from within you."

> Kasan said, "Learning by study is called hearing;
> learning no more is called nearness; transcending
> these two is true passing."

Kasan is certainly a master as far as finding exact analogies
from the experience of no-mind to the world of mind.
Nobody surpasses him. You have to understand him slowly:
Learning by study is called hearing. Somebody else has written, you have studied it; somebody else is teaching, you have
studied him – but it is all only hearing, it is not experience.
Knowledge cannot be converted into experience. On the
contrary, it is the greatest barrier to experience. *Learning by
study is called hearing.*

He says that at the most the studious, the learned can be
said to be people who have heard it. Not that they have
known it.

Every Buddhist scripture starts with the words, "I have heard…." There are thousands of Buddhist scriptures, but without any exception, every scripture begins with the words, "I have heard" – a deep sincerity, a truthfulness. "Buddha may have known, but as far as I am concerned, I have only heard."

Learning no more is called nearness. If you stop this kind of knowledge, if you drop this kind of knowledge, learning no more, Kasan calls it nearness. You have come very close; still, it is not experience. Learning was very far away; not learning is nearness, but even nearness is too far away.

Transcending these two is true passing. If you can transcend knowledge and you can also transcend no knowledge…in other words, if you can transcend ignorance and wisdom both, you have really passed to the beyond. This is called *true passing.*

> A monk asked,
> "What is 'true passing'?"
> Kasan said, "Beating the drum."

Nivedano…

> The monk asked again, "What is the true teaching of the Buddha?"
> Kasan said, "Beating the drum."

Nivedano…

The monk asked once more, "I would not ask you about 'This very mind is the Buddha,' but what is 'no mind, no Buddha'?"
Kasan said, "Beating the drum."

Nivedano...

The monk still continued to ask: "When an enlightened one comes, how do you treat him?"
Kasan said, "Beating the drum."

Nivedano...

This "beating the drum" of Kasan is a tremendous device. He says, "All your questions, howsoever great they look, howsoever profound and philosophical, they are all coming out of an emptiness within you." He is saying, "Just for a moment think of yourself as a drum."

That was his meditation to his disciples. If you can conceive of yourself as emptiness enclosed by the body, you will have understood the absurd action of Kasan. It is not logical; in fact, a logical person will think this man is mad. And by the way, Nivedano *is* – otherwise, why are you beating the drum?

Nivedano...

Good!

Setcho's commentary is not great, but still good.

> Dragging a stone, carrying earth,
> Use the spiritual power of a thousand-ton bow.
> Zokotsu Roshi rolled out three wooden balls;
> How could they surpass Kasan's "Beating the Drum"?

Different masters in different ages have used different devices just to take you out of your mind process, just to silence you, just to make you aware of your inner emptiness. Setcho said, "No other master has been able to surpass Kasan's beating the drum."

> I will tell you, what is sweet is sweet,
> What is bitter is bitter.

He is saying, "Kasan is simply concerned with the ultimate truth of your emptiness. Out of your emptiness all kinds of sounds, thoughts, imagination, dreams...but a good hit on your coconut..."

Nivedano...

Yeah, it hits well – many people seem to realize the emptiness!

Even if nobody else becomes enlightened, Nivedano's drum is going to become enlightened. That is not a small matter.

A few other Zen masters' statements before I come to Maneesha's questions:

> Kyuho said, "Our late teacher said, 'You should be completely finished up, emptied away; one nen, one eon; you should be like cold ashes and the dead tree, like the incense burner on the deserted shrine, like the frozen lake, like a piece of glazed silk.' Tell me, what does this mean?"
> The head monk said, "It means the realm of one color" – that is, great enlightenment.
> Kyuho said, "You do not understand our teacher's meaning."
> The head monk ordered someone to fetch a packet of incense and said, "If I cannot pass away while this incense is burning, your words will be proved true." He threw the incense into the burner. A cloud of white smoke rose, and while it still hung in the air, the monk passed away sitting up straight.

Kyuho, stroking the dead monk's back, said, "You
could pass away sitting up straight, but you could
never dream of our late teacher's meaning."

This passing away seems to be so miraculous. As the
incense will be burned away, the monk is saying, "I will be
gone with the smoke." That is the meaning of inner emptiness: "I can empty out myself any moment" – and he did
manage it, sitting straight; as the incense stopped burning he
was gone.

But Zen is a very strange way of approaching the truth.

*Kyuho, stroking the dead monk's back, said, "You could pass
away sitting up straight, but you could never dream of our late
teacher's meaning."*

This is going to be very hard. He has proved that he can
empty himself – so much so that he can die out of his own
will. As the incense burns and the smoke cloud moves away,
he will be gone. Still Kyuho said, "You have not understood
the meaning of beating the drum."

Why is he so hard about the poor fellow who has even
died, emptied himself completely? He is hard because he is
saying, "You have tried self-will by moving away your consciousness from the body like the smoke of the incense; you
have made a great effort of the will, and in fact your will is
your ego. You can do this, but you have not understood the
meaning of beating the drum. You have emptied yourself,
but you are there; you have proved yourself, but you are
there.

"In your very proving you have proved only your ego,
your power of will. You cannot understand the great meaning of beating the drum. It has to be relaxed. It has not to be
done by you because it is *there*. You have not to do anything,

you have simply to relax into it. You don't have to die, you have simply to be aware that emptiness is your innermost reality."

That's why although Kyuho seems to be hard on the poor fellow who has died, he is right: the man who has died must have had a great willpower.

I have told you about Nansen....

Before he was going to die, he informed all his disciples to come to partake in the ceremony of his death. He had thousands of disciples and he asked them, "Now please, anybody – suggest to me some original way of dying. I don't want to be in any way orthodox – I have never been in my life. Why should I be orthodox in dying if I have not been in living?"

The disciples looked at each other. Nobody had heard about an original death; death is death. Still, one suggested, "I have heard about a monk dying sitting, cross-legged, in a lotus posture."

Nansen said, "Stupid! So many have done that; it is nothing new. Just try to find something new. You are my disciples and you cannot do even this much for me? – to find an original way of dying? Do you want me to die like everybody else, lying on the bed?"

The bed certainly is a very dangerous place. Ninety-nine point nine percent of people die there…so beware! When the light is put off, simply get out of the bed – it is the most dangerous place. Be somewhere else: in the bathroom, on the floor, on the roof…anywhere, but avoid the bed.

Nansen said, "I am not going to die in the ordinary way."

Somebody suggested, "Then you can die standing up."

Nansen said, "That seems to be a little better, but still it is not unique, because I have heard about one Zen master dying standing."

That gave a clue to a disciple; he said, "That gives me an idea. Why don't you try it? Die standing on your head!"

He said, "This is great!" – And he stood on his head and died.

Now the disciples were at a loss what to do, because there exists no ritual for a man who has died standing on his head....

Somebody suggested, "His sister...she is his elder, she is a nun in the nearby monastery; it is better to call her. It is a dangerous case. We should not take any responsibility for it!"

The sister was called. She was older than Nansen; Nansen was ninety and the sister was ninety-five, but the sister was in no way inferior to Nansen in her understanding. She gave a hit to Nansen and told him, "Your whole life you have been mischievous; at least in your death behave!"

So Nansen jumped up, lay down on the bed, smiled – and died.

The disciples could not believe it, whether he is still dead...because first he had deceived them by standing on his head. "We would have burned him alive. Now it is better to wait for two or three days and see if he is really dead."

Nansen opened his eye and said, "I am really dead! There is no need to wait. When I am saying it who are you to dispute it. Is it my death or yours?"

They said, "Certainly it is your death."

So he said, "Can I close my eyes?"

They said, "It is up to you."

He closed his eyes and the disciples had to burn him, feeling very much worried – perhaps they are burning him alive or...who knows? He looks absolutely dead, but he looked dead when he was standing on the head, he looked dead when he was lying on the bed...!

Zen is certainly a very original way of living, of loving, of dying, of expressing its experiences.

Nivedano…

Have you got the feel of beating the drum?

There is nothing inside, still…it makes so much noise. Just look within yourself. What is there? A heartbeat, breathing coming in and going out…and what else? When you are utterly silent you are pure emptiness. Emptiness breathing…emptiness full of the dance of the heartbeat.

This is what is called going beyond, passing beyond – beyond knowledge, beyond ignorance – into the world of no knowing.

Maneesha has asked, "Would you agree with Kasan – that there is a state beyond learning?"

Kasan is not saying that there is a state beyond learning. Kasan is saying there is a *space* beyond learning, not a state but a space – infinite, empty.

Just watch this silence. Feel it, be drowned in it. And you will have tasted something of Zen.

These anecdotes are not ordinary stories. Each anecdote carries a whole scripture.

Her second question is: "Is it possible to hear through the eyes and see with the ears? That's what feels to be happening during these discourses.

"Would you please comment?"

Nivedano...

When one is absolutely silent, yes, one can see through the ears and one can hear from the eyes. Then there is no distinction between the senses, one simply becomes one sensitivity. Eyes and ears and nose, they all dissolve into one sensitivity. You see it, you feel through it, you hear through it – and still you remain silent. All this knowing from the ears and all this hearing from the eyes does not disturb your silence.

Yes, Maneesha, that's what I have been trying for years: to create the situation for you – and I feel immensely happy that you have responded with great rejoicing.

You have become part of this cosmic silence.

This is your true reality.

In this reality you are not.

And her third question: "What did the monk mean by his last question? To speak of how to treat a buddha sounds as if one has some control over how one will be in his presence, as if there might be a certain protocol to be observed. Would you please explain?"

You have completely misunderstood Kasan's answer. When asked, *"When an enlightened one comes, how do you treat him?"* Kasan said, *"Beating the drum."* It is not a question of any protocol; it is not a question of any control on your part. Kasan's approach has to be understood. Whatever your question is – this time it is meeting the Buddha – you may have asked, "If a buffalo comes by, how has it to be treated?" His answer would have been the same: "Beating the drum."

By this "beating the drum," he is saying, "All is empty, even the Buddha – he is far more empty than you. The only difference between him and you is that you think you are not empty, and he knows that he is empty and you are empty."

Try to understand Kasan more existentially than intellectually. He is not a man of intellect. He moved around with his drum, but he is certainly a great master. Language does not work. There is no other way to convey, but Kasan has invented, found a way – in an empty drum. You ask him or you do not ask him, he is going to beat the empty drum.

Kasan had thousands of disciples. Very few people can be said to have made more beings enlightened than Kasan, and he never spoke. His only speech was beating the drum.

Beautiful were these people and great must have been the people who followed and understood.

Golden were the days when even a Kasan could be understood. He was as awakened as any Gautam Buddha.

Now, Nivedano, the last beat on the drum....

Now the drum should be allowed to rest. And specially for the drum, I am going to tell a few stories:

Teddy Bearson gets the feeling that his wife is cheating on him, so he hires Mr. E.T. Pickle, the private detective, to follow her. Pickle has instructions to make a video film of all his wife's suspicious activities.

A week later Pickle reports: "Here it is!" He says, "All the evidence in living color – and with your best friend, too!"

Teddy and Pickle watch the movie together. Teddy's wife and his best friend are having lunch, swimming, dancing, walking and laughing in the countryside, making love under the pine trees....

"I can't believe it! I just can't believe it!" says Teddy.

"You better believe it!" says E.T. "The evidence is all here."

"That is not it," sighs Teddy. "I just can't believe my wife can be so much fun!"

Mabel Mince goes into the police station and tells the police officer that her boyfriend is missing.

The cop starts to fill out a report and asks Mabel if she can give a description of the missing man.

"Sure," says Mabel. "He is thirty-five, six foot tall, blond hair, blue eyes, very handsome and well mannered and he plays the guitar."

A friend of hers whispers in her ear, "Hey, Mabel, what are you talking about? Your boyfriend is short, fat and hairy!"

"I know," snaps Mabel, "but who wants *him* back?"

A man in New York is charged with hitting a woman on a double-decker bus, and the judge is asking him if he has any excuse.

"Well, Your Honor, it was like this," explains the man. "She came on the bus and sat next to me downstairs. Then she opened her bag, took out her purse, closed her bag, opened her purse, took out a dollar, closed her purse, opened her bag, put back the purse, and closed her bag again.

"Then she saw that the conductor was going upstairs, so she opened her bag, took out her purse, closed her bag, opened her purse, put in her dollar, closed her purse, opened her bag, put back her purse and closed her bag again.

"Then she saw the conductor coming down the stairs again, so she opened her bag, took out her purse, closed her bag, opened her purse..."

"Stop!" shouts the judge. "You are driving me crazy!"

"Right!" says the man, "That's what happened to me!"

Leroy and Liza, the black lovers, are out on a small country road, riding double on Leroy's old bicycle.

Suddenly they get the urge to make love. So there and then they jump off the bike and go for it.

After a few minutes a huge truck comes over the top of the hill. The driver sees the black couple rolling around in the middle of the road, so he gives a blast on his horn and frantically steps on the brakes – but Leroy and Liza just carry on making love.

The truck finally skids to a halt about three inches from the sweating couple. The driver jumps out of his cab and screams, "You crazy niggers! You could have been killed!"

Leroy lifts up his head, looks at the driver and says, "Well, I was coming, Liza was coming, and you was coming. And I figured, Hell, *you* was the only one with the brakes!"

Now two minutes for absolute silence.

No movement.
Close your eyes and collect your whole energy inward.

Now relax...

Okay, come back.

DRAGONS DO NOT LIE IN PUDDLES   15

Osho,

Chokei and Hofuku Discuss the Buddha's Words
Chokei one day said, "Even if you say that the arhats still have three poisons, you should not say that the Tathagata has two languages. I do not say that the Tathagata has no language but that he does not have two languages."
Hofuku said, "What is the Tathagata's language?"
Chokei said, "How can a deaf person hear it?"
Hofuku said, "I know you are speaking from a secondary principle."
Chokei said, "What is the Tathagata's language?"
Hofuku said, "Have a cup of tea."

Setcho's commentary is:

Who speaks from the first,
Who from the second principle?
Dragons do not lie in puddles;
Where dragons lurk,
Waves arise when no wind blows.
Oh! You, Chokei Zen monk
You've bruised your head on the dragon gate.

Osho,
With three pounds of drums, she pecks on the lotus
leaf. Knowing a spiral when she hears one, she'll be
beaten anyway.

My mind is coming to the boil! It is compelled to try
and decipher these stories, even though that feels
like reading the epitaph on one's own gravestone. So
I get my mind out, use it, give up, and put it away.
Then I get it out again, give up and put it away. Then
it gets out, uses me, gives up and puts me away.
I'm going insane or going in Zen! Help!
No, don't – keep doing it!
Or don't stop not doing what you don't do!
Osho, I take my head off to you.

Maneesha, before Nivedano beats his drum and Niskriya
cuts your head, I have to explain a few things of which

you may not be aware.

First is the word *arhata*. It simply means one who has overcome the enemies. In a better version, from where it is derived, it is called *arihanta*, which makes it clear that it has not only overcome the enemies: *ari* means the enemy and *hanta* means one who has murdered.

And what are the enemies? There are three enemies: covetousness, anger and folly.

In India, Hinduism is the *sanatan*, the eternal religion. One knows not when it started, who started it. Out of Hinduism, as a rebellion, two other religions have been born: one is Jainism, another is Buddhism. Jainism believes only in arhatas. Their word for it is *arihanta*; they don't know anything of the *bodhisattva*. The attitude of Jainism is, once a man has killed all the enemies – greed, jealousy, anger, lust – then there is no point for him even to speak a single word; he has nothing to convey. If anything is conveyed, it is conveyed by his presence. He is just like a well. If you are thirsty you go to the well, the well is not going to go running after you.

Perhaps this was one of the reasons Jainism remained a very small religion. Although it has a very refined, sophisticated philosophical understanding, it has had no masters; it had only *arhatas*. They have achieved and their work was done. Compassion was not compulsory. Why should they bother about anybody's misery, suffering, darkness? Everybody anyway has to fight it on his own; you cannot force anybody to be enlightened. What is the point?

Jainism has created many *arhatas*, great pinnacles of consciousness, but it has a very dry approach, a very inhuman approach. It does not consider at all those who are still struggling with darkness, blindness, who are still finding the path, who may be even going astray. The moment a man becomes an *arhata*, he cuts all his relationships with humanity, even the relationship of having a disciple.

Gautam Buddha created another rebellion which culminated finally in Zen. It differed from Jainism only on this point: it brought a new concept, *bodhisattva*. A *bodhisattva* is one who has realized his being, who has become awakened, but his work has not ended; on the contrary, now his real work begins. Up to now he was struggling for himself, now he will struggle for others.

According to Gautam Buddha – and I agree with him totally – a man of enlightenment cannot resist the temptation to encourage others to seek...to enhance, to support, to enrich and to share his own light with others. It is simply impossible for him.... The Jaina attitude seems to be very self-centered: you have arrived, your work is finished.

The story will help you to understand better...

Gautam Buddha dies and at the gates of paradise there is great celebration, because very rarely...in millions, perhaps one person comes to such a great peak of consciousness that the doors of paradise open for him. It is symbolic. And there was great rejoicing to welcome him, but he refused to enter the gate.

He said, "Please, close the gates. I will stand outside. Until every living being has passed inside, I cannot come in. I am going to be the last. Although it is a long waiting, I will wait. My love says I can wait, my compassion says I should wait. It is cruel on my part, when others are just to be awakened, not to awaken them but enter into the luxuries of paradise. I will come, but I will be the last. You please keep the doors closed." And the story is, the doors are closed; Buddha is standing outside, waiting for every human being to pass by.

That is the meaning of *bodhisattva*. Your achievement is not enough if you cannot share it. The more you can share it, the more you have it; the more you can spread the flame, the more hearts you can put on fire, the greater is your enlightenment. The *arhata* is compared to a small boat in which only he can sit, the *bodhisattva* is compared to a great boat in which many millions can be carried to the further shore.

There are many names for the *bodhisattva* according to the dimension in which the word is used. One of the names is *tathagata*. *Tathagata* comes from the root *tathata*. *Tathata* means suchness, thisness; everything is here and everything is now. There is no past and there is no future; and in your suchness, in your nature, you are already enlightened. *Tathagat* means one who conceives every being as enlightened: a few are aware of it, a few are not, a few want to play the games of life a little more. A few are attached to their teddy bears, but sooner or later one gets rid of the teddy bear. A *tathagata's* approach is to make you aware that what you are clinging to is just dream stuff. If you want to cling you can cling, but remember, there is nothing to cling to.

I told you the Jaina proverb that the thirsty will come to the well, but the well is not supposed to run after thirsty people. Gautam Buddha's statement parallel to it is, "If the mountain cannot come to me, I will go to the mountain! Obviously it is difficult for the mountain to come to me, but that does not mean that the mountain has to miss me. I will go."

This small anecdote is concerned with Buddha's words, and for centuries – twenty-five centuries – his words have been discussed by great masters. Such beauty has blossomed in those words, such rainbows have come out of those words. Gautam Buddha in this sense is very rare. No other person in the whole of history has been commented on by so many and has been showered with so many new meanings. He is certainly alone.

Chokei, another *bodhisattva*,

> ...one day said, "Even if you say that the arhats still have three poisons..."

He is not saying they have, he is saying, *"Even if you say that the arhats have still the three poisons..."* of covetousness, anger, folly; still...

> "...you should not say that the Tathagata has two languages."

It has been argued again and again between masters. For the contemporary world these beautiful statements, commentaries, have lost their meaning. But unless they are revived, something in you will remain missing. They are so essential to human spirit and its growth.

He is saying that a *tathagata* cannot be said to have two languages. There have been masters who have said that a *tathagata* has two languages. So first you have to understand...otherwise, Chokei will not be understood.

Those who have said a *tathagata* has two languages have their own meaning. A *tathagata* has to speak with those who do not know and a *tathagata* has also to speak to those who know. Obviously he needs two languages. When you are with one who knows, you use one language, and when you are with someone who does not know, you have to use a different language.

But Chokei says, "You can say if you want, that the

arhatas still have three poisons – which is impossible, because an *arhata* becomes an *arhata* by overcoming those three poisons." You can say that – Chokei allows it – but you cannot say about the Buddha, about the Tathagata, that he has two languages: "*I do not say that the Tathagata has no language, but that he does not have two languages.*"

Chokei is saying something immensely important. On the one hand he says,

> "I do not say that the Tathagata has no
> language, but…"

I certainly say that he has not two languages.

> Hofuku said…

Hofuku is another Zen master – and this is traditional in Zen that masters meet and talk and play with words:

> Hofuku said, "What is the Tathagata's language?"

If you say he has not two languages and you don't deny him having any language, then what is his language?

> Chokei said, "How can a deaf person hear it?"

This is such a beautiful statement with so many implications. I am speaking to you, but do you think if you don't have ears I will still be speaking? My speaking needs you absolutely.

It is one of the latest scientific discoveries…philosophers have always been discussing it, but their discussions do not have scientific validity. But science has now come to see a point which puzzles the ordinary man. For example: you all have different colors of clothes, but if the light is put off, do you think the white will remain white and the blue will remain blue, the red will remain red and the green will remain green? Once the light is off, all colors disappear. For the colors to be there, the light is needed. And things become more complicated: light may be there, colors may be there, but if there is nobody to see, there will not be any color; the eyes are also needed. These are basic components.

So when you leave your room and lock it, don't be surprised that everything in your room has changed its color! All has become colorless. But if you look just from the keyhole, again the colors will appear. So it is very difficult to find your room without seeing it! Once you see, things are there – and once you stop seeing, they disappear. Your eyes are needed.

Just look at it this way. A blind man, do you think that for him there is any such thing as color or light? A rainbow may be there, but it is not for the blind man. The stars may be there in the sky, but they are not for the blind man. Great music may be there, but if you are deaf it does not exist for you – and if everybody else is also deaf – then sound does not exist.

You can understand it; our range of seeing is very small, so is our range of hearing. Right now you don't hear any radio station. All around the earth thousands of radio stations are broadcasting, and those waves are passing by your side. They are available to your ears, but your ears' range is not so deep that it can catch them.

It happened in the Second World War. A man got a bullet in his head, the bullet was removed, but something happened within his brain system that he started hearing the nearest radio station without any radio, perfectly well and correctly.

First he was puzzled. There is no radio around and he can hear every statement, the time and the songs and everything. He said to the doctors – he was still in the hospital – that something was strange. Nobody believed him, because it had never happened.

But finally they had to try – at least hypothetically try. In another room they put a radio, and one doctor was there taking notes. Another doctor was with the patient taking notes of what was going on in the radio broadcast. They were surprised. He was absolutely accurate.

You might think that it was a great thing; he should have enjoyed! Nobody can enjoy it for twenty-four hours, because there is nothing, no way to put it off. He could not sleep, he could not talk, because the continuous radio broadcast was going through his head. He could not hear people properly. He was going crazy. His ear had to be operated on.

But that gave an insight that although all kinds of waves are passing by – radio waves, television waves…your net is just small and it does not catch them. Either they are above it or they are below it.

What we see is just a small range of things. The blind man cannot see the light, but do you think the blind man can see darkness? Ordinarily it is presumed that a blind man must live in darkness; you are wrong. The blind man cannot even see darkness, because he has no eyes to see. If you can see darkness, there is no problem in seeing light, because light and darkness are one phenomenon. Close your eyes and it is dark; open your eyes and it is light. Don't think that the blind person is just like you, because you close your eyes and you see darkness. The same is not the situation of the person who is born blind, because he has nothing to compare it with – he has never seen light. How can he say, "This is darkness"?

> Hofuku said, "What is the Tathagata's language?"
> Chokei said, "How can a deaf person hear it?"

He is saying that only those who are not deaf know the language of Buddha. Those who are deaf may hear his words but will not understand his language, will hear his words but will not understand the meaning – most probably will *mis*-understand his meaning.

> Hofuku said, "I know you are speaking from a secondary principle."

You have to see why Hofuku said, *"you are speaking from a secondary principle."* The first principle is: Buddha is speaking; the second principle is: somebody else is listening. If you are speaking from the standpoint of the listener, then you are speaking from the secondary principle. That cannot be accepted. "Speak from the first principle, from the original source. I am not asking about whether people hear Buddha or not, I am asking whether Buddha speaks or not."

> Chokei said, "What is the Tathagata's language?"

Again the same question. Unless you speak from the original source, Chokei is going to ask again and again,

> "What is the Tathagata's language?"
> Hofuku said, "Have a cup of tea."

This answer – *"Have a cup of tea"* – means listen to a buddha or become a buddha. It simply means have a taste of it, don't talk about it. It is not a question to be discussed, it is something to be experienced like taste: "Have a cup of tea!"

This statement, "Have a cup of tea," comes in many Zen anecdotes from different directions.

A professor of philosophy went to see Nansen and he asked about great things: God and heaven and hell, and the ultimate truth, and time and space; he was full of words. Nansen listened and said, "Wait. First have a cup of tea."

The professor felt a little offended. He is asking such great questions and this fellow brings in a cup of tea! Naturally he said, "Don't change the subject!"

Nansen said, "I am not changing the subject, I am bringing you to the subject." He prepared the tea, the professor sipped the tea and Nansen asked, "Can I ask you how it tastes?"

Naturally the professor said, "You can taste for yourself. Taste cannot be discussed."

Nansen said, "You are a nice fellow. Some day perhaps you will understand. At least you are not an idiot. These ultimate truths, the meaning of nirvana and the meaning of enlightenment...you can't even express the taste of tea and you are talking about enlightenment?"

Religion in the East has never become a theology. It has remained very earthly, very grounded, very pragmatic. And particularly Zen never wavers; it brings you back to the experience. Nothing can be said about the experience. All that is being said is only a net to drag you into the experience. What is said is not true, it is just a pointer showing you the way to where you may find the truth.

It is said about Mahavira – both he and Buddha were contemporaries – that he never spoke, but there are scriptures in which Mahavira's words are collected. Still, it is said he never spoke. It looks absurd but you have to understand the intricacy of the thing. Mahavira certainly never spoke. He had no great assemblies as Gautam Buddha had. He had only a very small group of chosen people who could understand his silence.

He has not written a single word. Those eleven people whom he selected as his listeners, without his speaking, have written the scriptures. It is a miracle that all those people have written the same thing. Certainly they understood the silence.

Silence itself is a language; it just needs a very silent heart, an empty heart to understand it.

Mind is not the right mechanism to understand great things. It is useful for the mundane, but for the sacred, for the divine, it is simply a hindrance; hence the emphasis of the East on meditation. Meditation is nothing but by and by dropping the mind and coming to a point when you have no mind at all.

In that space of no-mind you can hear a master – who may not be speaking at all, or if he is speaking, then you will be able to understand him. You cannot misunderstand him.

Setcho's commentary is:

> Who speaks from the first,
> who from the second principle?
> Dragons do not lie in puddles.
> Where dragons lurk,
> Waves arise when no wind blows.
> Oh! You, Chokei Zen monk
> You've bruised your head on the dragon gate.

Setcho has not been able to say anything special. He is

simply saying that just as dragons do not lie in puddles, the great buddhas cannot be found in words.

When no wind blows, no waves arise, there is understanding. Then you have come to the first principle, the source. Do not talk about the second principle, because that is irrelevant. There are as many second principles as there are listeners, but the first principle is one.

Maneesha has asked… Choosing the sutras for these discourses she is getting a little taste of Zen: "Osho, With three pounds of drums, she pecks on the lotus leaf. Knowing a spiral when she hears one, she will be beaten anyway."

So now two things have to be done: first, Master Niskriya, she has spoken something right so give her a reward.

[*Niskriya touches Maneesha's head with his staff and Maneesha bows down to Osho in gratitude.*]

Good. And now Nivedano…

Declare to the world with your drum, three times…

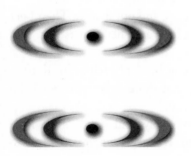

Good.

She is saying, "My mind is coming to the boil! It is compelled to try and decipher these stories even though that feels like reading the epitaph of one's own gravestone."

You are right, Maneesha, I don't have here a cup of tea – but still you can have a cup of tea. It will not be visible…but from my eyes, from my gestures, from my presence, have a taste. There is no need to be worried about your gravestone.

Walking on the path of Zen is walking toward the greater death, consciously, finding one's own grave.

Everybody dies, but just as people live unconsciously they die unconsciously. Neither has their life any meaning and significance nor their death. Once you start becoming a little aware…just a small awareness, a small candle flame, and you can see your own death every moment. And beyond your death – the eternal life.

Death is an episode. It happens millions of times, but it is not able to destroy the living energy that you are.

And I can understand your difficulty. You are saying: "So I get my mind out, use it, give up, and put it away. Then I get it out again, give up and put it away. Then it gets out, uses me, gives up and puts me away.

"I am going insane or going in Zen! Help! No, don't – keep doing it! Or don't stop not doing what you don't do! Osho, I take my head off to you."

Zen is certainly a very crazy way. Unless you are a little crazy, you won't come to Zen. It is true, when you come to

Zen, your craziness will go through an alchemical change. Your insanity will become your greater sanity, your no-mind will become your tremendous wisdom.

But from the outside it is crazy. From the inside it is the only sane thing that has happened on this planet.

Maneesha has made you too silent. I would like your silence to be deeper and the only way to make it deeper is to have a good laugh.

Little Felix is having a test from a child psychologist.

"Now, Felix," says the shrink, "what do you want to be when you grow up?"

"I want to be a doctor, an artist, or a window cleaner," replies Felix.

"I see," says the puzzled shrink, "you're not very clear about it, are you?"

"What?" says Felix. "I am perfectly clear. I want to see naked women!"

Old Mrs. Grumblebum was going every day to visit her doctor. The doctor – a very patient man – humors her, listens quietly and sometimes gives her medicines.

One day Mrs. Grumblebum doesn't show up. The next day the doctor asks, "Where were you yesterday? I missed you."

"I'll tell you the truth," she replies, "I was sick!"

At the latest summit talks, Ronald Reagan and Mikhail Gorbachev are continually arguing about whose country is number one, Russia or America.

Finally, in order not to start the third world war, they decided to settle it between themselves by running a marathon race.

The next morning at eight o'clock, the two world leaders start the race. Two and a half hours later, Gorbachev happily passes the finish line, but it is another six hours before Reagan makes it. He is utterly exhausted, but not beaten yet.

The following morning the *Washington Post* runs the story: "In a very dramatic marathon race our great president came in an excellent second. We hear that Gorbachev also participated, but he came in second to last."

An English woman and her young son are traveling in a taxi in New York. As the taxi drives down 42nd Street, the boy is fascinated by the heavily made-up ladies walking along the street, accosting male passers-by.

"What are those ladies doing?" asks the boy.

His mother blushes and says, "I expect they are lost and are asking people for directions."

The taxi driver overhears this and says in a loud voice, "Why don't you tell him the truth? In other words they are prostitutes."

The English woman is furious, and her son asks, "What are prostitutes? Are they like other women? Do they have children?"

"Of course," replies his mother, "that's where New York taxi drivers come from!"

Three young Catholic girls want to join a nunnery, but it is a very strict order so the girls have to pass an interview before they are admitted.

Mother Superior calls the first girl and asks her, "What would you do if you were stopped by a man on a dark night?"

"I would kneel down and pray to Jesus," replies the girl.

"Good," says the head nun turning to the second girl. "And what would you do?"

"I would scream and shout for help," replies the girl. "Good," says the Holy Mother turning to the last girl who looks very young and innocent. "And what would you do, my dear?"

"I would pull down the man's pants," replies the girl. "Ah, dear!" cries the Mother Superior almost in a faint. "And what would you do then?"

"I would pull up my skirt," she replies.

"Jesus Christ, save us!" croaks the old nun. "And then what?"

"Then," says the girl, "I would run like hell!"

Now, close your eyes.
For two minutes just be absolutely still,
as if frozen.

Relax…

Okay, come back.

Osho,

Tanka's Have You Had Your Dinner?
Tanka asked a monk, "Where are you from?"
The monk replied, "From the foot of the mountain."
Tanka said, "Have you had your dinner?"
The monk said, "I have had it."
Tanka said, "Is he open-eyed who brings food to a fellow like you and lets you eat it?"
The monk could make no reply.

Later Chokei asked Hofuku, "To give food to others is surely worthy. How could he fail to be open-eyed?"
Hofuku said, "Both giver and receiver are blind."

Chokei said, "Are you still blind, even though you exhaust every means?"

Hofuku said, "How can you call me blind?"

Setcho's comment is:

Exhaust every means, and you will not be blind;
You hold the cow's head to let it graze.
The Four Sevens, the Two Threes,
The following band
Have handed down the dharma treasure,
Raising dust and trouble to make men drown on land.

Osho,
It seems to me that Zen provokes responses from
one's intuition, though I'm not even quite sure what
intuition is. Is there a connection between Zen and
intuition?

Osho,
I have heard that Gurdjieff used to serve up food to
his disciples and watch them overeat and become
drunk in response. You are serving up such delicacies in these evenings it feels that we need to refine
our palettes and select the right implements before
we can hope to savor what you make available.

The anecdote, which concerns Tanka's asking a monk,

"Have you had your dinner?"

Is a way in Zen to ask someone, "Have you got it? Are you fulfilled? Has contentment happened to you? Are you awakened? Is your being enlightened?" Zen uses ordinary words like dinner and raises them to heights unimaginable.

> Tanka asked a monk, "Where are you from?
> ...Have you had your dinner?"

In Zen you are coming from nowhere and you are going to nowhere. You are just now, here, neither coming nor going. Everything passes by you; your consciousness reflects it but it does not get identified. When a lion roars in front of a mirror, do you think the mirror roars? Or when the lion is gone and a child comes dancing, the mirror completely forgets about the lion and starts dancing with the child – do you think the mirror dances with the child? The mirror does nothing, it simply reflects.

Your consciousness is only a mirror. Neither you come, nor you go. Things come and go. You become young, you become old; you are alive, you are dead. All these states are simply reflections in an eternal pool of consciousness.

Unless you understand it, these anecdotes will look absolutely absurd.

First asking him, *"Have you had your dinner?"*

If you met Tanka – and Tanka is one of the rare Zen masters – what will you answer to him? You will not even understand what he means by dinner. Zen has developed a special language of its own: *"Have you had your dinner?"*

The monk remained silent. Perhaps he could not understand: "What does he mean? – is he asking me, inviting me for dinner?" What kind of inquiry, when you meet someone – suddenly, the first question, "Have you had your dinner?"

Seeing the monk, Tanka had asked, *"Where are you from?"* It is an effort of Tanka to provoke the man to understand the language.

> "Where are you from?"
> The monk replied, "From the foot of the mountain."

He missed. He is not asking about the place from where you are coming, he is asking the ultimate question: "From where is your consciousness coming? Do you understand that you are endless, that you are not coming from anywhere, you simply are?"

Tanka said, "Have you had your dinner?"

Tanka is asking the monk another question to give him an opportunity to understand. Dinner does not mean dinner, it simply means, "Are you fulfilled? Are you complete in yourself? Have you found your center? Are you nourished by existence? Have you found your home?"

> The monk said, "I have had it."

The poor fellow is still thinking about dinners, but out of his great compassion, for which he is known....

> Tanka said, "Is he open-eyed who brings food to a fellow like you and lets you eat it?"

Encountering a Zen master means encountering a lion. He will hit you from this side and that side, from this point and that point.

[*Suddenly everyone is thrown into darkness as the power fails.*

276

Some timeless moments of silence with Osho before he continues with the discourse.]

Now, asking the monk, "Is he open-eyed – is he an awakened person, is he enlightened – who brings food to you? Have you got a master who nourishes you?" But strange language. And strange were those days and strange were those people. *"Is he open-eyed who brings food to a fellow like you and lets you eat it?"*

The monk could make no reply.

He cannot understand what is going on. Now he is completely puzzled and confused. All this talk about dinner seems to be about something else.

Later Chokei asked Hofuku, "To give food to others is surely worthy. How could he fail to be open-eyed?"

An ordinary understanding is that to give food to those who are hungry, to feed them, is a virtuous act. Obviously such a virtuous act can be done only by one who is awakened. At this point the Catholics and other Christians will certainly agree with Chokei, who is saying, *"To give food to others is surely worthy. How could he fail to be open-eyed?"*

In such ordinary statements so much is hidden. It is possible for you to feed the hungry and yet not be awakened. You can feed the hungry for reasons of your own. Most probably it is because of greed – greed for heaven, for heavenly pleasures. If you can accumulate enough virtue, you will be received by God. And if you are not virtuous, a sinner, a hellfire is waiting for you into which you will be thrown for eternity; there is no rescue.

Ordinary morality will agree with Chokei, but anyone who understands the meaning of inner awakening knows it perfectly well: to feed someone does not mean a virtuous act because it is coming out of unconsciousness, out of greed, out of a certain motivation, certain ambition, certain fear. How can you be called an awakened person? The awakened also feeds, but not because of any profit to be gained here or hereafter. The awakened also feeds not only the body but the soul, out of pure compassion, never expecting anything in return.

Hofuku said, "Both giver and receiver are blind."

These are great dialogues between great people. Chokei himself is enlightened. You might not understand his asking, "How could such a man *fail to be open-eyed, who feeds others?*" This is a net thrown to catch Hofuku. If Hofuku said, "Yes, you are right," he would have missed the point, but Hofuku stands on the same ground as Chokei. He makes the statement, *"Both giver and receiver are blind"* – to think that "I am giving" is ego-centered and to think that "I am receiving" is also ego-centered. There is no difference; both are blind.

Chokei said, "Are you still blind, even though you exhaust every means?"
Hofuku said, "How can you call me blind?"

Before we think about Setcho's comments, something more about Tanka has to be understood, because this dialogue is about Tanka asking a monk, *"Have you had your*

278

dinner?" and *"From where are you coming?"*

Who is this fellow Tanka? He stands as high as any enlightened person has risen, ever – and with a uniqueness of his own.

> Tanka was a contemporary of Nansen, Ryutan, Ho
> Koji and Yakusan...

All great masters, but none of them had the extraordinary quality of Tanka. He first studied Zen with Basho.

Just to study with Basho is enough to give you a new way of seeing things. Just to sit by his side is enough to make you unique. Basho is one of the great awakened ones. Basho stands in the history of Japan, just as in the history of India, Gautam Buddha stands; the same height, the same peak, and something more. Basho was also a mystic, a poet, a painter. The very fact that he accepted Tanka as his disciple is in itself a certificate of uniqueness. Basho was not for the masses, he was only for the chosen few.

> ...and then at Basho's suggestion, Tanka went
> to Sekito.

Sekito was very lonely, without any disciples, a mystic living deep in the mountains. A few times Basho sent a few disciples to Sekito because he could see that they needed a different kind of nourishment. With Basho they would become enlightened, but just to be enlightened is not enough. To be enlightened and still remain unique needs a certain atmosphere, a different kind of air.

This is something to be understood about Zen. In no other religion does one master send his disciples to another master, never. In all the religions of the world every master is a competitor to other masters. They are fighting for disciples because whoever has more disciples is a greater master. It is sheer politics, politics of numbers – although their game is religion, hidden behind the word *religion* is pure politics.

Sekito was very averse to disciples. Just to avoid them he had gone far away deep in the forest. But Basho could see in Tanka some similarity, something that can fall in deep harmony with Sekito. There is no competition. It is not a question that you have more disciples, so you are great. Zen masters continually send people to other masters.

That is a rare phenomenon: no competition, and on the other hand, a deep understanding of the disciple. If Basho sees that "somebody else can help Tanka more than I can help, because he does not belong to the same kind of energy," then it is better not to prevent him and waste his time but send him to the right man.

> Tanka lived with Sekito three years and finally returned to Basho's temple. Before paying his respects to Basho, he went into the monk's hall and climbed up onto the shoulders of a statue of Manjushree.

Manjushree is one of the disciples of Gautam Buddha, the first disciple who became enlightened; hence, his status is just next to that of Gautam Buddha. The monk I have told you about who became enlightened sitting under the tree, and flowers showered and showered, was no one but Manjushree.

Now this was very strange of Tanka, coming back to the temple of Basho where Manjushree's statue is worshipped.

Basho loved Manjushree, felt some synchronicity between himself and Manjushree. Tanka went into the temple and climbed up onto the shoulders of Manjushree.

> The monks were astonished and went to tell
> Basho, who came down to the hall. He saw Tanka
> and said, "My son, Tennen."
> Tanka climbed down from Manjushree's shoulders
> and made bows to Basho, saying, "Thank you
> master, for giving me my dharma name." And
> thereafter he was called Tennen, meaning son
> of nature.

Tanka is another formation of Tennen.

Rather than being angry with him, rather than being offended, "What kind of nonsense are you doing? It is insulting to Manjushree and it is insulting to me!" Instead of saying that, he said, "My son, Tennen." He has initiated him with such love – "My son" – and has also given him the name Tennen.

> Tanka climbed down from Manjushree's shoulders
> and made bows to Basho, saying, "Thank you
> master, for giving me my dharma name."

These kinds of anecdotes you will not find in any religious tradition around the world. What was the meaning of Tanka climbing up on the statue of Manjushree? In this gesture he is declaring without saying a single word, "I have reached higher than Manjushree. Do you recognize it or not?"

Basho recognized it. He said, "My son, come down. You will be known as Tennen." To give the dharma name, the name of sannyas, is to accept the disciple.

It was also Tanka who features in the story about using a wooden statue of Buddha to burn in a temple one night to keep himself warm.

The night was cold, and in Japan there are wooden statues. When the priest went to sleep – Tanka was just a guest; the night was cold – he took one of the statues of Buddha and burned it. Now this would be utter disrespect by anyone anywhere in the world – but not in the world of Zen, and you will see why.

The priest was awakened, seeing that in the temple there is a fire. And when he reached, he could not believe his eyes – he was only a priest – he said, "Are you mad? You have burned the statue of Buddha!" Tanka took his staff and started looking into the burnt ashes of the statue for something.

The priest said, "What are you looking for?"

He said, "I am looking for the bones of Buddha."

The priest said, "You are really mad! This is a wooden statue; wooden statues don't have bones."

Tanka said, "You are a very intelligent man, you have understood. Just bring another statue! The night is long and very cold, and you have so many statues...and rather than taking care of a living buddha, you are bothering about a wooden buddha. What do you want? A living buddha should shiver in the cold and wooden buddhas should sit on their thrones?"

The priest thought that this man should not be left alone – he would burn those statues and they were very valuable. But now he has proved his point: how can wood be a buddha? You can carve it into a statue of a buddha, still it is wood. Buddha is inside you. He was saying to the priest,

"Here I am, and you are preventing an awakened man from burning ordinary statues."

The priest pushed him out of the temple and locked the temple door. Tanka said many times, "This is not right. You are not behaving as you should."

He said, "I don't want to listen to anything, just get out! I cannot leave you alone inside the temple, and I am going to sleep – I am not going to waste my whole life sitting, watching that you don't do any stupid thing."

In the morning, when the priest opened the door of the temple, he said, "Certainly this man *is* mad." Because Tanka was still sitting by the side of the road, where there was a milestone. He had plucked a few wild flowers and put those wild flowers on the milestone and he was worshipping, doing his morning meditation. He said, "In the night you burned a buddha and in the morning you are worshipping a milestone! Have you any sense?"

Tanka opened his eyes and he said, "If wood can be a buddha, stone can also be a buddha; it is just uncarved, the buddha is hidden. It needs a sculptor and the buddha can be found. I can see buddha is in this stone. The buddha that I burned in the night must have been just a wooden log and some artist must have carved it. This is raw material; it can become a buddha. And the question is not...I am not concerned about the wood or the stone, I am concerned about buddhahood, which is the nature of everything. I am a buddha, you are a buddha.... In the night a living buddha burned a dead buddha, in the morning a living buddha is worshipping a dead buddha for the simple reason that nobody worships this poor buddha. Out of compassion, at least give him satisfaction that one man recognized his innermost being."

> Further, it was noted about Tanka that when he
> was eighty-one years old, he retired to his temple
> at Mount Tanka in Hunan province.
> One day four years later, he said to his disciples,
> "I am starting on my journey."
> He equipped himself with hat, leggings, socks and
> staff, and put on a shoe. Before his foot hit the
> ground, he was dead.

Can you see the man? What a great man! He is going on the eternal journey, so he is getting ready.

This is why Zen masters ask again and again, "Suggest some original way of dying." Now this is an original way, equipping himself with hat, leggings, socks and a staff, and putting on a shoe. Before his foot hit the ground he had died. He has left everything behind; his consciousness has moved on the great pilgrimage.

If you understand Tanka, then it will be easy for you to understand his questioning… *"Have you had your dinner?"*

He was not an ordinary man.

> "Where are you from?"

He must have frightened the monk. He said: *"From the foot of the mountain." Tanka said, "Have you had your dinner?" The monk said, "Yes, I have had it." Tanka said, "Is he open-eyed who brings food to a fellow like you and lets you eat it?" The monk could make no reply.* He is saying, "Have you been a disciple, a learner? Have you drunk from the sources of an awakened being? Have you eaten from the sources of truth and love and peace?"

Now Setcho's comment is:

Exhaust every means, and you will not be blind.

Once in a while, he comes with a right answer. *Exhaust every means*; whatever you can do, do.

And when you cannot do anything, you will find yourself.

Make every effort, exhaust all means, because unless you exhaust all means, a lingering doubt will remain in your mind: "Perhaps if I had gone on this way, I would have reached." So go on all the ways, exhaust every possibility, eliminate every effort. Come to a point where you can be effortless, where you don't know what to do. In this non-doing, in this let-go, in this relaxation you will find your own self blossoming in its immense glory and splendor.

You hold the cow's head to let it graze.

He is asking, "Do you hold the cow's head to let it graze? If the cow is there and the grass is there, the cow is going to graze, you just wait. You are there, your longing to know yourself is there, just wait!"

The Four Sevens, the Two Threes,
The following band
Have handed down the dharma treasure,
Raising dust and trouble to make men drown
on land.

A beautiful statement. *The Four Sevens* are the twenty-eight Indian patriarchs, beginning with Mahakashyapa – they are called the Four Sevens. *The Two Threes* are Chinese patriarchs, beginning with Bodhidharma. *The following band*...after that, in Japan, hundreds of monks became enlightened. Now there is no question of numbers; it is called simply "the following band."

They all have the same experience of enlightenment, but still there are differences and those differences are very minute and very delicate.

For example in a dark room with one candle, the room is full of light. With two candles the room is full of light. With three candles the room is full of light. With four candles the room is full of light. You go on increasing the number of candles, the room is still just full of light. What one candle can do will be done by a hundred candles, nothing more, because light may become more and more bright but its intrinsic quality of dispelling darkness is the same.

Hence I have said to you, just the taste of a single dewdrop and you have known all the oceans.

But Setcho is for the first time making a very loving statement: The four sevens, the two threes, and the band following *have handed down the dharma treasure.* They have been handing down the experience of truth, *raising dust and trouble to make men drown on land.*

Naturally this will explain to you why Jesus is crucified, why Socrates is poisoned, why Al-Hillaj Mansoor is stoned to death. These people create trouble.

I am condemned all over the world. You may understand; you may not understand. Twenty-four countries will not unnecessarily bother about a man who never leaves his room. Still, two years after I left America, their parliaments are discussing whether the law should be withdrawn, or the law should be kept, which prevents me from entering in their countries. Just two days ago the parliament of Germany decided to continue to keep their law – I am still alive....

But what is the fear? These people, Setcho says, create

great trouble. First they make everybody aware of their ignorance. That is a great trouble. You may have cancer, you are
not aware of it. You are perfectly happy going fishing but the
doctor creates the trouble. He says, "You have cancer and
you don't have much longer to live."

Where are you going? Are you still going to go fishing?
Now the whole desire, the whole joy of going fishing is finished, you return home with a sad face. It is not the cancer
that has made your face sad, it is the doctor.

When a Gautam Buddha arises, he creates so much trouble in so many people's minds, in so many people's families,
in so many people's hearts. He is a trouble-maker because he
goes on telling you, knocking on your doors, that you are
fast asleep while if you wake up you will find a great treasure
hidden in you. All misery and all agony will disappear;
ecstasy will be your reward. Blessings will shower on you.
But wake up!

Anybody who wakes you up seems to be like an enemy,
even in ordinary waking. Early in the morning, when the
breeze is cool and you would like to have another turn and
hide yourself in the blanket and somebody goes on pulling
your leg – "Get up, it is time for meditation!" – how do you
feel? You feel like killing this man! And if you don't listen to
him, he starts the Dynamic Meditation then and there in
your room. Anyway he won't allow you to sleep.

Setcho is right. These people create so much dust where
everybody is so peaceful in his agony, everybody is so happy
with his troubles – where everybody is living in utter stupidity but without any questioning, without any quest. These
people come and they shake you: "What are you doing? You
are not meant to do these things. This is not your destiny,
this is not what you are keeping hidden within yourself. This

is not the flower and the fragrance of your being."

Naturally the category of the buddhas has always been condemned, poisoned, killed. Every effort has been made somehow – these people should go and do their Dynamic Meditation somewhere else: "Why do you disturb us? We are sleeping well – although we are suffering from a nightmare and a migraine. But we are well acquainted with that; we have always suffered with migraine so there is no problem in it."

But these people say, "You are talking about a migraine; we are telling you to drop the mind itself. With the mind the migraine will also go. Without mind you cannot have a migraine."

Nobody has been able to do it up to now, to have no mind and just migraine. But without a migraine it will look so lonely. It has been such a good friend, such an old acquaintance, always with you. Wherever you go it has followed like your own dog, and now somebody says, "Get rid of this dog." You cannot feel that it is possible. Nobody believes that a buddha is possible.

In the presence of a buddha one becomes enchanted, one becomes full of trust that certainly there is a possibility, a new opening of existence and a new experience of life. But as you go home, just on the way, one after another doubts start arising…perhaps that man has hypnotized you. Perhaps with so many people listening so silently, you got caught in their silence. Alone the migraine is back; alone the old doubts are back. People avoid….

Just a few days ago I had an infection in the ear and Doctor Jog, the best expert in Pune, was called to see me. He came. He could not believe that here are thousands of people with such a joyful, playful aliveness, caring about the garden, meditating or just sitting silently, doing all kinds of work, but without any anxiety.

He told me, "You will have to forgive me."

I said, "For what?"

He said, "I had many times passed by the gate. The gate attracts, but the mind says, 'Beware! Everybody inside is hypnotized.' Your name is such that if I talk to anybody about you, he looks at me as if I am a little bit crazy."

On the second day he brought his wife. The third day they came to listen, and he told me on the fourth day, "I told the people of my profession outside, the other doctors, that our conception is absolutely wrong, and they should go and see with their own eyes what is happening here: a great experiment in consciousness. It is so tangible; the silence is so expressive, and the bliss. You can almost feel it in the air, in the atmosphere." They all said to him, "Jog, you are lost. Don't go there again! You are hypnotized, we can see."

And he told me, "The people of my profession started avoiding me just because I have been treating your ear."

And when he came with his wife he asked me, "My wife wants to see you alone for five minutes."

I said, "Perfectly okay" – and I am waiting. Both have disappeared. Jog must have been afraid that if the wife becomes too much interested in my caravan then she is gone! And there are examples of people...

Another doctor, Dr. Modi has lost Zareen. Zareen is here; Dr. Modi is sitting alone in a vast house. A nice and good man, he comes to the ashram – and a man of understanding. He has not created any trouble for Zareen. She wanted to come to the ashram; he allowed her, and he still comes to the ashram. But everybody in his profession must be telling him,

"Look, that is what happens. You have lost your wife. Why in the first place have you taken her there? Whoever goes inside the gate somehow disappears."

I do nothing at all, and parliaments in different countries are discussing for hours whether I should be allowed into their countries and I have never asked them! I don't want to go anywhere. I have made it clear to everybody, "Don't be afraid. I am not going anywhere" – but who knows...?

They are keeping a law that I cannot even step outside at their airports; entering the country is out of the question. I cannot even step out at the airport! What is the fear? Certainly, I must be creating some trouble in their minds.

I am creating trouble. Their lives are settled and whatever I say is going to unsettle their lives. Nobody wants to be unsettled, nobody wants to be left alone by the crowd. Such a fear exists that even my own centers...Jayantibhai must be here; yesterday he was. Ahmedabad center has asked, "Can we drop your name from the center's name, because your name creates trouble."

It is *my* center, but because of my name nobody wants to come there. So I told them, "You drop my name. Let people come. My name is not important; my message is important."

Tanka has created the right silence. I will take Maneesha's question some other day. Today there is just a little time for having a good belly laughter. We receive and welcome this silence with our laughter – and our laughter helps to open deeper doors of silence and mystery.

A black man is having a conversation with God: "Tell me, Lord," he says, "how come I am so black?"

"You are black," replies God, "so that you can withstand the hot African sun."

"Tell me, Lord," continues the black man, "how come my hair is so short and kinky?"

"So that you will not sweat in the hot African climate," replies God.

"Tell me, Lord," implores the black man, "how come my legs are so long?"

"So that you can escape from the wild beasts that roam the jungles of Africa," replies God.

"Then tell me Lord," shouts the black man, "what the hell am I doing in Chicago?"

"Noah!" booms the voice of God.

"What?" shouts Noah looking around. "What do you want?"

"You have got to take one of those elephants out and bring in another one."

"What for?" shouts Noah.

"Because," booms the voice, "you have got two males and you need one male and one female."

"I'm not bringing nothing in!" shouts Noah. "You just change one of them."

"Come on, Noah," booms the voice, "you know I don't work like that."

"Well, I'm sick and tired," says Noah, "I have had enough of this. I have been working for days. I am through with it!"

"Noah?" asks the voice

"Yeah!" shouts back Noah.

"Noah," comes the voice, "how far can you swim?"

Hamish MacTavish goes salmon fishing and at the end of a long day he catches a tiny fish, not even big enough for one mouthful. Hamish is just about to kill the fish when it speaks to him.

"Hamish MacTavish!" gurgles the fish, "I am a magical fish, and if you spare my life I will grant you three wishes."

"That's great!" says Hamish.

"But," continues the fish, "because you are such a mean old Scotsman, remember, everything you ask for, your worst enemy Fergus MacPherson will get the double."

"Okay!" agrees MacTavish, "I would like a fortune in gold!"

"Done!" gurgles the fish, "But MacPherson gets the double."

"And," continues Hamish, "I would like a dozen beautiful women for my pleasure."

"Agreed!" gurgles the fish, "But MacPherson gets two dozen!"

"Okay," says MacTavish, grinning, "and my last wish is for you to painlessly remove one of my balls!"

It is a closely guarded secret that the Vatican has a weekend resort for senior church members.

The nuns who live in this special resort are sworn to silence, but they have worked out their own coded language.

One weekend, the resort is graced by His Holiness Pope the Polack, along with a cardinal and a bishop. After dinner the three men of the church retire to their rooms where they are entertained by their hostesses.

The following morning at breakfast, Sister Margaret, who has been entertaining the bishop, picks up a piece of toast and with a great display butters it four times.

Sister Gloria, who has spent the night entertaining the cardinal, takes her toast, and with a satisfied smile, butters it five times.

Sister Theresa has spent the night in Pope the Polack's room, and looks a little pale and tired. Slowly, she reaches for her toast. She takes some butter, and spreads it three times.

The other two nuns start to giggle. But then, Sister Theresa turns her toast over, and butters it three times on the back.

Now close the eyes.
Be absolutely still – no movement.
Just gather all of your energy within.

Now let go.

Okay, come back.

JUST FALL LIKE A BAG OF RICE   17

Osho appears tonight after an illness of many days – one of several periods of weakness and ill health he has suffered since his incarceration by the American government in 1985.

During the last two weeks, a new meditation therapy has been launched, with "Zen Master Niskriya" leading the pilot group. It is called the "No-Mind Meditation," and consists of a week-long program of an hour of gibberish followed by an hour of silent watching.

Tonight, Osho brings gibberish to the assembly, establishing a new format for the nightly meditations at the end of each talk.

My Beloved Ones,

I am introducing you to a new meditation. It is divided in three parts.

The first part is gibberish. The word *gibberish* comes from a Sufi mystic, Jabbar. Jabbar never spoke any language, he just uttered nonsense. Still he had thousands of disciples because what he was saying was, "Your mind is nothing but gibberish. Put it aside and you will have a taste of your own being."

To use gibberish, don't say things which are meaningful, don't use the language that you know. Use Chinese, if you don't know Chinese. Use Japanese if you don't know Japanese. Don't use German if you know German. For the first time have a freedom – the same as all the birds have. Simply allow whatever comes to your mind without bothering about its rationality, reasonability, meaning, significance – just the way the birds are doing.

For the first part, leave language and mind aside. Out of this will arise the second part, a great silence in which you have to close your eyes and freeze your body, all its movements, gather your energy within yourself.

Remain here and now.

Zen cannot be understood in any other way. This is the last part of the series *Live Zen*.

In the third part I will say, let go. Then you relax your body and let it fall without any effort, without your mind controlling. Just fall like a bag of rice.

Each segment will begin with the drum of Nivedano. Before Nivedano gives the drum, there are a few more things I have to say to you.

I am extremely sorry that I have not been physically here for many days, but I am also extremely happy that you never missed my presence.

I was in your heart
and I was in the wind and in the rain
and the thunder of clouds.
I was in your tears,
in your nonsense utterances....
I was absolutely present here with you –

and those who are present know it perfectly.

I was absent only for those who themselves are absent. At least today, don't go anywhere.

Nivedano, give the first drum...

ishtciamistrasimbaworrrastaba
coslnusmarpatokulospos **SHARNAS**
MBHALASRHADDABASLAMKAMALKALEJAKAM
σηαβναστιασκι λυλαβελαβαλλαβαρ
wiurnci**LULABELABALLABAR**
khellkerstaticlagnonjdt tjkn khjjknhhuzdgugfurrlasma
sleikniylokjdlaih
srubbililisisrirtra jkh kijkadponolo gerrastas
waslagugru

[Everyone bursts into a sea of sound, volume and tempo clashing and crashing in one great crescendo – a tidal wave of mind.]

[Osho motions to Nivedano for the second drumbeat]

[An instantaneous silence falls over the whole auditorium.]

Now the third drum…Relax…

The fourth drum…Come back!

This begins and ends the series called *Live Zen*.
What I could say, I have said to you.
What I could not say, I have given to you.

ABOUT THE AUTHOR

Osho defies categorization, reflecting everything from the individual quest for meaning to the most urgent social and political issues facing society today. His books are not written but are transcribed from recordings of extemporaneous talks given over a period of thirty-five years. Osho has been described by *The Sunday Times* in London as one of the "1000 Makers of the 20th Century" and by *Sunday Mid-Day* in India as one of the ten people – along with Gandhi, Nehru and Buddha – who have changed the destiny of India.

Osho has a stated aim of helping to create the conditions for the birth of a new kind of human being, characterized as "Zorba the Buddha" – one whose feet are firmly on the ground, yet whose hands can touch the stars. Running like a thread through all aspects of Osho is a vision that encompasses both the timeless wisdom of the East and the highest potential of Western science and technology.

He is synonymous with a revolutionary contribution to the science of inner transformation and an approach to meditation which specifically addresses the accelerated pace of contemporary life. The unique OSHO® Active Meditations™ are designed to allow the release of accumulated stress in the body and mind so that it is easier to be still and experience the thought-free state of meditation.

OSHO INTERNATIONAL MEDITATION RESORT

Every year the OSHO International Meditation Resort welcomes thousands of people from over 100 countries who come to enjoy and participate in its unique atmosphere of meditation and celebration. The 28-acre resort is located about 100 miles southeast of Mumbai (Bombay), in Pune, India, in a tree-lined residential area set against a backdrop of bamboo groves and wild jasmine, peacocks and waterfalls.

The basic approach of the resort is that of Zorba the Buddha: living in awareness, with a capacity to celebrate everything in life. Many visitors come to just be, to allow themselves the luxury of doing nothing. Others choose to participate in a wide variety of courses and sessions that support moving toward a more joyous and less stressful life by combining methods of self-understanding with awareness techniques. These courses are offered through OSHO Multiversity and take place in a pyramid complex next to the famous OSHO Teerth zen gardens.

You can choose to practice various meditation methods, both active and passive, from a daily schedule that begins at six o'clock in the morning. Each evening there is a meditation event that moves from dance to silent sitting, using Osho's recorded talks as an opportunity to experience inner silence without effort.

Facilities include tennis courts, a gym, sauna, Jacuzzi, a nature-shaped Olympic-sized swimming pool, classes in zen archery, tai chi, chi gong, yoga and a multitude of bodywork sessions.

The kitchen serves international gourmet vegetarian meals, made with organically grown produce. The nightlife is alive with friends dining under the stars, with music and dancing.

Make online bookings for accommodation at the new OSHO Guesthouse inside the resort through the website below or drop us an email at guesthouse@osho.com

Take an online tour of the meditation resort, and access travel and program information at: www.osho.com/resort

The daily meditation schedule may include:

OSHO® Dynamic Meditation™: A technique designed to release tensions and repressed emotions, opening the way to a new vitality and an experience of profound silence.

OSHO® Kundalini Meditation™: A technique of shaking free one's dormant energies, and through spontaneous dance and silent sitting, allowing these energies to be redirected inward.

OSHO® Nadabrahma Meditation™: A method of harmonizing one's energy flow, based on an ancient Tibetan humming technique.

OSHO® Nataraj Meditation™: A method involving the inner alchemy of dancing so totally that the dancer disappears and only the dance remains.

MORE OSHO BOOKS

Over 7000 hours of talks by Osho have been transcribed into books. If you go to www.osho.com you can sort the titles by subject so you can choose the books that interest you most.

ENLIGHTENMENT: THE ONLY REVOLUTION
Talks on the Great Mystic Ashtavakra

Powerful and penetrating talks on the famous dialogue between the mystic Ashtavakra – one of Osho's favorite ancient Indian masters – and King Janak. By the end of the dialogue, King Janak is enlightened. Says Osho, "There are no other statements anywhere as pure, transcendental and beyond time and space as these."

ISBN 81-7261-070-X
ISBN 978-81-7261-070-8

THE PATH OF MEDITATION
A Step by Step Guide to Meditation

"Become a watcher of thoughts, but not a thinker." A guide to meditation: How to prepare the body, mind and emotions for meditation. An invitation to experiment with powerful techniques. Illustrated with black and white photos from the meditation camp in Mahabaleshwar, India, where these talks were given.

ISBN 81-7261-071-8
ISBN 978-81-7261-071-5

THE SEARCH
Talks on the Ten Bulls of Zen

The ten paintings that tell the famous Zen story of a farmer in search of his lost bull provide an allegorical expression of the search for enlightenment.

Osho examines the deeper layers of meaning behind each painting. He also talks about the relation between discipline and awareness, and about the path of love and the path of meditation and where they meet.

ISBN 81-7261-188-9
ISBN 978-81-7261-188-0

I AM THE GATE

This is the book in which Osho talks about himself – not as a man, not even as a mystic, but as a manifestation of existence itself.

This book is a timeless classic that has served as an introduction for many people to Osho's vision. Eight discourses to push the reader over the edge of the intellect into the mysterious, the esoteric and the transcendental.

Osho talks on the meaning of initiation, disciplehood and meditation – a loving invitation to begin the journey toward the ultimate truth: "A sannyasin to me is a person who decides to live to the utmost, to the optimum, to the maximum; it is just like a flame burning from both the poles." A helpful reader for those new to the world of Osho.

ISBN 81-7261-199-4
ISBN 978-81-7261-199-6

MEDITATION: THE ART OF ECSTASY

In a series of talks especially of help for the beginner, Osho clears up the misconception about the relationship of concentration to meditation. He also underscores the point that meditation is not a serious business; on the contrary it opens up the dimension of lightheartedness, joy, play and creativity within each person.

Making meditation immediately accessible for everyone, Osho suggests a variety of techniques specially designed for today's seeker. He also provides detailed descriptions of each stage of his own revolutionary meditation technique, Dynamic Meditation. The last section of this book describes other radical meditation techniques by Osho.

ISBN 81-7261-000-9
ISBN-978-81-7261-000-5

NOWHERE TO GO BUT IN

These days, where spirituality is on everyone's mind, it is difficult to distinguish between borrowed words and jargon and sincere existential questions from people who are trying to understand themselves and their lives.

In this book you will see how Osho guides people away from asking superficial "religious" questions to opening up and exposing their reality in real questions. His answers are not academic, they do not fill the questioner with secondhand knowledge, but provide existential responses which take us to a new level so that we can get in contact with our own understanding and experience.

ISBN 81-7261-017-3
ISBN 978-81-7261-017-3

THE PATH OF THE MYSTIC
In Search of the Ultimate Freedom

Throughout this book, Osho emphasizes the imperatives of individual freedom and of seeking and living the truth. Among the tools he offers to travelers on the mystic path are the dynamic yet subtle combination of meditation and hypnosis, methods for exploring past lives, and the Bardo – the ancient Tibetan instructions for the dying.

He outlines his liberating, radical vision for a new humanity – awakened beings who are a synthesis of the worldly, earthy Zorba the Greek, and the silent, witnessing Buddha. Readers are challenged to step beyond the limits imposed on them by their social, religious and political conditioning, and to bring about the global transformation that can only begin at the most personal, individual level.

ISBN 81-7261-204-4

ISBN 978-81-7261-204-7

FROM SEX TO SUPERCONSCIOUSNESS

Osho speaks on the need and the way to understand sex in its deepest sense, thereby transforming it. The life energy that flows into sex is the same life energy that becomes superconsciousness, enlightenment. This book is a detailed description of the way this transformation happens.

"There is a religious experience, a spiritual experience involved behind the craving for sex. If we can become aware of that experience we can go beyond sex."

ISBN 81-7261-010-6

ISBN 978-81-7261-010-4

FOR MORE INFORMATION

www.OSHO.com

a comprehensive multi-language website including OSHO Books, talks (audio and video), a magazine, the OSHO Library text archive in English and Hindi with a searchable facility, and extensive information about OSHO Meditation techniques.

You will also find the program schedule of the OSHO Multiversity and information about the OSHO International Meditation Resort.

The original recordings of the talks in this book can be downloaded from osho.com/audiobooks.

To contact OSHO International Foundation go to: www.osho.com/oshointernational

OSHO International Meditation Resort
17 Koregaon Park
Pune 411001 MS, India
resortinfo@osho.net

To order OSHO Books,
CD's and DVD's within India, contact:
OSHO Media International,
17 Koregaon Park, Pune 411001
Tel: +91 (20) 6601 9981
email: distribsale@osho.net
For all other orders, go to osho.com/shop
for a list of overseas distributors.